FLYING WITH BISCUIT BOMBER BOB

THE UNTOLD STORY OF WWII AIR TRANSPORT IN THE PACIFIC

by

Robert R. Mosier
with
Beverly Mosier

Dockside Sailing Press

2014

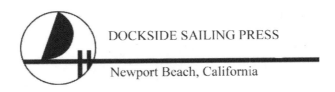

DOCKSIDE SAILING PRESS

Newport Beach, California

Printed in the United States of America.

Dedicated to my lovely wife
Beverly, my lifelong partner.
Working together we finished this book.

Special thanks to Nancy C. Swan, my daughter,
for her encouragement, text editing, photographs,
and art work.

Loving support from all my family members
has kept the book's progress alive
—Robert R. Mosier

CONTENTS

FOREWORD xi

EDITOR'S NOTE.. xiv

PART I:

MAP: Western U.S. Pilot Training Command Locations xvi

CHAPTER 1 Origins 1

CHAPTER 2 Earning My Wings................................. 11

CHAPTER 3 The Home Front..................................... 17

PART II:

MAP: Aircraft Delivery, Troopship Route, U.S. - New Guinea . 24

CHAPTER 4 On to New Guinea 25

MAP: New Guinea/Biak/Peleliu/Philippines 34

CHAPTER 5 Move to Biak 35

CHAPTER 6 Overloaded Take-off............................... 41

CHAPTER 7 Life on Biak 47

CHAPTER 8 Troop Carrier Missions 59

CHAPTER 9 Glider Towing 65

CHAPTER 10 Peleliu Island 71

PART III

MAP: Philippines to Okinawa 80

CHAPTER 11 Move to the Philippines: 81

CHAPTER 12 Air Rescue at Santo Tomas 85

CHAPTER 13 R and R in Australia.............................. 89

CHAPTER 14 Life in San Jose: Supplying Guerrillas 99

CHAPTER 15 Luzon: Porac and Clark Field 105

PART IV

MAP: Okinawa to Japan 116

CHAPTER 16 Okinawa: Japan Surrenders 117

CHAPTER 17 First Flight to Tokyo 123

CHAPTER 18 Hokkaido Rescue: We "Capture" an Airfield 127

CHAPTER 19 Tachikawa, Japan 131

PART V

Home, Family, Career 144

CHAPTER 20 Homeward Bound 145

CHAPTER 21 Life Resumed 149

CHAPTER 22 An Inventive Career 165

CHAPTER 23 Epilogue 177

APPENDIX: How to Fly a Transport Aircraft 181

                   Return at Your Leisure 188

ANNOTATED BIBLIOGRAPHY 189

END NOTES: 194

ACKNOWLEDGEMENTS AND CREDITS 197

INDEX 199

ILLUSTRATIONS

1. Bob High school xiii
2. "Biscuit Bob" xiii
3. Bob, Craig & Bev work in View of Pacific Ocean xv
4. Observatory from Bob's House, Hollywood Sign Behind 3
5. Crystal Beach Gang, Gymnast Bob Top of Pyramid 4
6. Bob's Brother, Jack Mosier. 4
7. Beverly Christiansen. 6
8. Bob in Cockpit of a Basic Trainer. 12
9. AT-17 Forced Landing, Douglas Arizona 14
10. The Three Sisters Learn to use Guns 16
11. WWII Era Radio Dominates Room against Wall, Beverly on R. 16
12. Victory Garden, Peas and Chickens 18
13. P-38. 21
14. Beverly Age 14 22
15. Bob's Sister, Mary Mosier 23
16. *USS General R.E. Callon Troopship.* 25
17. New Guinea Native. 30
18. Bob and Other 57th Squadron Pilots 32
19. 10 in 1 Rations 33
20. "Biscuit Bombers" Drop Crates of Supplies. 33
21. Capt. Pennock in Intelligence Briefing Pilots. 37
22. C-47's Near New Guinea 38
23. 375th, and 57th Morale Patches designed by Disney 40
24. P-47 Fighter 46
25. Showers. 48
26. The Hospital on Biak 51
27. Bob and Friend find Paradise with Nurses 51

28. Jungle Rescue 55

29. Dispensary on Biak 56

30. Cliff visits Biak 57

31. Lurking Danger: Bob & Cliff discover child held a hand-grenade .58

32. Paratrooper Drop 62

33. Loading a Jeep in a C-47 63

34. C-47 Towing Glider 67

35. Troops in Glider Ready for Towing 67

36. Pilots used Maps, Instruments, Sight & Landfall Navigation . . 74

37. Japanese Cave Hideout 78

38. Tacloban, Leyte Island 81

39. Water Buffalo, called Carabao 83

40. University of Santo Tomas Internment Prison. 84

41. C-46 Evacuating the Nurses out of Santo Tomas 84

42. Santo Tomas Liberation 84

43. Highway as Landing-Strip, View toward the University & Manila .87

44. Typical Thatched Home Philippines 88

45. C-47s in Philippines 88

46. C-47s Flying over Manila 88

47. Nurses by C-46 91

48. C-47s Port Moresby 91

49. Wau Airstrip 92

50. Typical Thatched Home 94

51. Captain Pennock's Book 96

52. Farming with Carabao 99

53. Yontan Airfield Okinawa 105

54. Lingayan Gulf Airstrip 106

55. Clark Field 1945 107

56. P-47s, Floridablanca 108

57. Cliff & Bob, Clark Field 109

58. Army WACS 111

59. Flying over Nakagusku Bay Okinawa 113

60. Ie Shima Island 115

61. Kadena Airfield, Okinawa. 118

62. Naha, Main City on Okinawa, Wiped-Out after the Fighting. . 119

63. Hiroshima in Ruins. 123

64. Army DUKW, aka Duck. 138

65. Hiroshima after the Bomb. 139

66. The Air Medal 143

67. Bob and Collins Radio Apollo Team 144

68. Little Church of Hollywood Wedding 155

69. Collins R390A Radio 162

70. Main Street, Richardson Texas 1950 167

71. Collins Radio Plant, Newport Beach, California circa 1959. . . 169

72. Collins Burbank Office 171

73. Collins Newport 172

74. Bob and Beverly 176

75. Typical Family Gathering at Home in Laguna Beach, CA. . . . 176

76. Beverly's P-38 Lucky Charm 179

FOREWORD

When I was a very young boy our father took my older brother, Jack, and me, to Mines Field in the Los Angeles area (presently Los Angeles International Airport) to visit the German Graf Zeppelin on public display celebrating the completion of its epic around the world flight. I was fascinated watching the local barn-storming bi-planes stunt flying over Mines Field. I knew I would just have to be an airplane pilot someday. Flying immediately became my life goal. At the time, I imagined it was an impossible dream.

Two major events occurred, one almost destroying the flying dream for good, the other making it a possibility.

The most important and saddest thing of my young life and most difficult to overcome, was that my father, the person who was so full of plans for his sons, college being the most important, fell sick from meningitis, went to the hospital one day and died never returning home.

The family was so suddenly deprived of his love, help and guidance that we suffered from both his loss and our own bewildering future plight. Jack, just out of high school, discovered that he must now take charge of our mother, younger sister and even me with only California welfare for family support. Going to work was his only choice as his other life-long dreams disappeared. I tried to help him by working as a paperboy for the Hollywood Citizen news while finishing high school.

The second event also changed everything.

The leaders of foreign countries across two oceans from our United

States had taken the world into war. We barely knew their names then, but those men changed everything—for nearly everybody! In no time it seemed that the entire World was at war and the outcome was very important to countries not yet involved, even ours.

My brother, now draft age, working on P-38 airplanes at Lockheed Aircraft Company, decided that he wanted to join the Army Air Force. He was hoping to become a pilot and indicated that I would be left at home to take care of our mother and sister. That got me thinking.

I had graduated from High School at age 18 but my own dream of flying suddenly looked like a real possibility and within my reach. I chose to volunteer for the draft myself, hoping I would also be accepted for flight training in the U.S. Army Air Force. That would give us two military checks to send home to Mom. With our sister Mary's own job at the Telephone Company they would be alright. The fact that I might get to fly an airplane after all, was the most importing thing to me at the time. This is my story; you are invited to fly along with me, Biscuit Bomber Bob.

My WWII activities as a very young troop carrier pilot from 1943 to 1946 involved adventurous flying missions from New Guinea in the South Pacific, all the way north to Japan. Along with thousands of others, I was constantly hopping from one remote island to another, always with the goal of bringing an end to the war by closing in on Tokyo.

The Nadzab, Papua New Guinea airport where I first became acquainted with the C-47 Troop Carrier aircraft had been captured with the aid of paratroopers dropped on the field to seize it from the Japanese. Planes took off from Port Moresby and Dobodura to accomplish that mission. This took place in September, 1943, a year before I arrived.[1] But it set in motion the planned, leap-frogging method of advancing towards our goal by delivering supplies to our combat troops on those remote islands by air. This was to become my life during the war.

Many, many years later, in 1995, I was asked to recall those days for one of my grandsons, who had been accepted into the Air Force Academy in Colorado Springs. It did not exist in my youth, nor did the

Air Force as a separate military unit. It was only established at the war's end in 1946.

As an assignment, the Air Force Academy had requested that the new cadets submit information about family members who had been in the military flying forces. My grandson's own goal was to become a pilot and he asked me to provide more details about flying and combat.

As I played my small part in a very large war, my missions allowed me to view many places along the route from the air and from the jungle below where fighting continued and dangers lurked. Those experiences grew me up in a hurry. The more I recalled about those stress-filled, but interesting days, the more the children and grandchildren wanted to hear. Even I often stopped in amazement at realizing what had been expected and delivered by my age group in that time of America's need. So at their constant insistence, I kept writing. My wife, Beverly, helped me to fill in my story with information that I had missed while overseas in the service. She was in California coming of age during those turbulent years of uncertainty when the men were away and maybe not coming home.

Though my Air Force days were long ago, many memories were enhanced by saved boxes of memorabilia including all my letters home lovingly bundled by my mother. The fact I still had them and they could be found, surprised even me. Once the memory flood gates were opened and my grandson in the Academy had what he needed, the other family members began to pester me for more of my WWII pilot stories. Writing was more work than I had anticipated, but I felt it was an important story to tell, Not just because it is my story, but because it is also the story of thousands of other unsung young men and women who served.

—Bob Mosier
Laguna Beach CA

Bob High school   *"Biscuit Bob"*

EDITOR'S NOTE

From a cliff over Fisherman's Cove in Laguna Beach, Bob and Beverly Mosier's home looks out at the Pacific Ocean towards San Clemente and Catalina Islands. The hillside beneath their balcony is bright with hundreds of rosebushes and overlooks a sandy beach below dotted with colored umbrellas of beachgoers. There are other flowering plants and hummingbirds swarm around the feeders they've hung from the eaves of their house. On days when the US Navy conducts live fire training exercises on San Clemente Island, the bay windows in their home rattle with the sound of distant explosions. On occasion they have seen the tracks of cruise missiles launched from ships out in the Pacific Ocean heading in towards the island and then turning north in the direction of the Naval Ordinance Test Station at China Lake, California.

With this view, it is not difficult to slip back to those long ago days in the South Pacific, to imagine dark steaming jungles, runways carved out of coral or lined with steel matting on a brown stripe carved through the green forest on some remote island. Their house is lined with mementos of that distant war. There are pictures of Bob piloting in the cockpit of a C-47 aircraft, ready to launch down the runway to deliver needed supplies to the fighting troops on the next island up the chain leading to Japan and to bring back the wounded from the latest battle fields. There are models of the various aircraft he has piloted and somewhere in the house a box with his U.S. Army Air Medal and various campaign ribbons.

Bob was 19 years old when he finished his flight training and was commissioned a second lieutenant in the Air Force. He celebrated his 20th birthday on a troopship sailing to New Guinea. Early on as part of the "Biscuit Bombers," nickname for the 57th Squadron, 375th Troop Carrier Group, he volunteered for every mission no matter what the weather was like, nor did he care much about the conditions where he had to land. He told me that initially he had a fatalistic outlook about the war—he did not think he would survive. He loved flying and decided he was going to get as much of it as he could while he was able. Later on, as he ferried troops and equipment from island to island and on to Okinawa and Japan, he changed his outlook.

He weathered the horrific typhoon that sank three U.S. ships and grounded or damaged hundreds of others. As time went on, he decided that he might actually survive the war and became a little more conservative and cautious about flying into heavy thunderstorms.

While this is Bob's story, it is also the largely unknown story of Squadron 57's "Biscuit Bombers," and the flight and ground crew members that kept the C-47s and C-46s in working order for fast response to deliver food rations, troops, and ammunition to the ground forces jumping from one South Pacific island to the next. Flying through bad weather to rude airstrips carved out of the jungle, they often landed under enemy fire to deliver their loads and airlift the wounded back to hospitals for treatment.

Bob epitomizes the thousands of young Americans who left their homes and undertook hazardous flying conditions in unarmed planes. This is just as much their story as his.

To his and our good fortune, he did survive the war, came home, encountered a beautiful woman a few weeks later, and three months after that, on his twenty-second birthday, they were married. From this union has come a distinguished cadre of four children, 14 grandchildren, and 14 great-grandchildren. After the war Bob entered college, got a degree in electrical engineering, and from that beginning he went on to a notable career in electronics, telecommunications and the burgeoning new field of computer science and digital communications. Besides his achievements as one of the "Greatest Generation," his engineering and scientific accomplishments have led to significant human benefits. There is no doubt in my mind that his talented offspring are continuing that tradition.

His story is moving and inspirational. I feel honored to have played a small part in making it available to a wider audience.

—Craig B. Smith
Editor

Bob, Craig & Bev work in view of Pacific Ocean

PART I

• ORIGINS • FAMILY • GROWING UP IN SOUTHERN CALIFORNIA
• FLIGHT TRAINING • OFF TO WAR • LIFE ON THE HOMEFRONT

WESTERN U.S. PILOT TRAINING
COMMAND LOCATIONS

andrewmizell.com

CHAPTER 1
ORIGINS

Bob: All during my younger years I dreamed of being a pilot. After Pearl Harbor these feelings were even stronger and now began to seem achievable. So in January 1943, after I graduated from John Marshall High School in Hollywood, California, I went to Los Angeles and found the military office where I took all of the tests to qualify myself for aviation training. After passing the physical and the written exams I received a letter testifying to that. Now, armed with this letter, I took the gamble and volunteered for the draft as they explained I must do to be considered for the Army Air Corps. On March 17, 1943, at age eighteen and a half, I was inducted by my draft board, and just as I expected, I was sent to the Santa Ana Induction Center as an enlisted man still hoping for acceptance as an Aviation Cadet and a pilot.

A little background: I was born in San Francisco on September 9, 1924, the second of three children. My brother Jack was born in 1921 and my sister Mary completed the family in 1925. My Dad, John Mosier, said he was born in Payne Junction, Iowa to a large family, the youngest of 14 children. He left home as a teenager and went to Canada where he became a fur trapper to make a living. Too young to serve in WWI, he went to San Francisco and became an auto mechanic. Mary Humburg, my mother, was part of a family of actors. Born in San Francisco, she narrowly survived the San Francisco earthquake of 1906 but her family records and most other belongings were lost to the resulting fire. Her family formed the Humburg Family Stock Company, which put on traveling plays. All of the actors were her mother and father Humburg and their five children, Edyth, Charlotte, Mary (my mother), Arthur and John and four grandchildren, Royal, Pat, Bob and Rodna. During WWI, Humburg, a German name, became unpopular, so they took the old English family name of Fletcher instead. They put on the successful plays across the country, in what was called at that time a "stock company." The whole family participated and they loved acting and dressing for the parts. However, eventually movies took over the theatres that they performed in and killed the business, so the family moved to Hollywood where they got involved in movie making. Or as they said, If you can't beat 'em…Join 'em! They would go to central casting and get hired on as extras for five dollars a day. My mother Mary had three children by then so she didn't participate as much, but stayed home with us. Some of her family got agents and performed speaking parts in films for many years.

I was two years old when the family moved from San Francisco to Los Angeles. We lived in a rented house in south Los Angeles, around 102nd street, in an area now called Watts. My Dad found a rental home high in the Hollywood Hills with a fantastic view, at 3922 Cumberland Avenue. Somehow Dad saved enough money to open two radio stores, (one located at Vermont and Beverly) where he sold those newly invented popular radios. That was where I first got interested in electronics, building crystal sets, and making antennas. Dad lost both stores during the depression. Then he often had to sell oranges on a street corner to support the family.

My elementary education was interrupted by the Long Beach earthquake of 1933. I was nine years old at the time, and Jack and I attended school in a makeshift tent for the next couple of years. Over 100 schools were damaged or destroyed by that earthquake. When the earth started to shake I was at home reading the Sunday comics. I thought the house was going to slide down the hill, but Dad comforted us, and luckily no one was hurt. Because our father only had an eighth grade education, he always stressed the importance of a college education, so we all worked harder in school for that reason. In addition, money was tight so we all did odd jobs to earn our own spending money. I followed in Jack's footsteps working as a newspaper boy. Starting at age 12, I delivered papers on my bicycle and then graduated to a more responsible position as a street sales manager.

Besides the fact that jobs were scarce, even worse, our dad became ill with tuberculosis. His health made working difficult. I was in second grade when Dad's health worsened and he had to enter Olive View Sanatorium in Sylmar, California. Without any means of support, our family had to go on welfare. After many months, when I was starting high school, Dad was able to return to work, and he succeeded in getting a job as an electrician working on installing the planetarium science exhibits at Griffith Park Observatory. That was when we were first able to buy our own house, close by at 3937 Cumberland Avenue, on that same high Hollywood hill. Dad joked that he could use one of the telescopes at the Observatory to watch me walking to school, just down the hill from the Observatory. He backed up this warning by telling me how he'd watched me kick a can down the street that morning. Later on Dad took a different job with the City of Los Angeles, working in the Controller's office.

View of Observatory from Bob's House, Hollywood Sign Behind

Our dad was a strict disciplinarian, and we were a close loving family looking after one another. He helped the boys with their paper routes by driving us when it rained, but pampered his only daughter. While working for the *Hollywood Citizen News*, I entered a contest based on gaining subscriptions to the paper. I walked the entire area and won a prize of a trip to Catalina Island. It was there in Avalon, on December 7, 1941, just having fun, when I heard that startling news of the Japanese attack on Pearl Harbor that led to a complete change throughout my world.

Before the change and the War, I always took part in school activities. I was a two-year letterman in gymnastics and was also a cheerleader. At that time only boys were cheerleaders at sports events; no girls were allowed. Besides college prep-required academic classes, I took auto shop just so I could learn to work on cars. I never got to own one but my brother Jack did. On some occasions I was allowed to borrow Jack's 1930 model A Ford, even though I crashed in it twice, once on Sunset Boulevard and another time near the high school. At the time, I was working as a pin setter in a 52 lane bowling alley on Sunset Boulevard. Coming home at 5 A.M. one morning after working all night, some guy coming from the opposite direction delivering papers turned right into me. I knew my brother would be mad at me, and I was equally mad at the guy who caused the accident. But as no one was hurt except for the car's dents, I had to go home and face the music. The second time a teacher ran into me near the high school. My brother was mad at me as expected, but I knew it was not my fault this time either.

Growing up, I basically was a good kid and tried to stay out of trouble. Still, I ended up in the Hollywood Police Station twice, but got off with warnings and was never booked. The first time was for driving by and whistling at girls and the second time was when my gang went to the Grauman's Chinese Theater. One guy bought a ticket and then opened the back door so the rest of us could sneak in, but we were caught. In high school I belonged to the "Crystal Beach Gang," a group of guys who liked to hang out and surf at Crystal Beach, which was located between Santa Monica and Venice beaches. The gang didn't have today's meaning then. It was just a friendly group of boys who hung out together at a malt shop near Hollywood and Vermont Boulevards, where we would meet our girlfriends, drink malts and listen to the nickelodeon.

Crystal Beach Gang,
Gymnast Bob Top of Pyramid

My brother Jack was graduating from high school when our Dad came home not feeling well. He was taken to the hospital, and the next thing we knew he was dead. This was in 1941, a few weeks before Pearl Harbor. It turned out he had spinal meningitis. There was no cure at that time, but it is treatable today. I was devastated, a terrible feeling of loss. My dad and I were very close. He'd been to my school to give talks about radios and astronomy. Our friends were shocked, too. I didn't know how our family could survive without him. Jack knew he had to take over supporting the family while I finished school. So he did. Once I graduated he immediately joined the Army. I was right behind him...or perhaps a little faster.

Bob's Brother,
Jack Mosier

With only a High School Diploma, I was inducted into the service at the Santa Ana Center and sent to Kearns Field, south of Salt Lake Utah for that extreme physical torture called Basic Training. By virtue of my letter of acceptance for the Air Force and by talking to senior Army personnel, I was lucky to be accepted as a potential Aviation Cadet. I was sent by train to attend the University of Denver where all the young cadets took classes in flight basics and celestial navigation, which thanks to my dad I knew a little about. I also made an effort to impress the girls on campus.

While in Denver I had my first exposure to flying in an Army single engine "Taylor Cub" type aircraft with a pilot. Then, returning to the Army Air Force Base (SAAAFB) in Santa Ana, California for pre-flight evaluation in order to judge my suitability for becoming a pilot, navigator, or bombardier, I was chosen as an Aviation Cadet for Pilot training. Wow! I was the happiest man alive when that happened. I was moving quickly, on a fast track to becoming a pilot as long as I could perform well. Primary training at Wickenburg Airfield in Arizona was the next stop and where we flew PT-17s and I did my first solo flight. Wickenburg was followed by basic flight training at Minter Field in the San Joaquin Valley near Bakersfield, California, which in turn was followed by advanced flight training school at Douglas Arizona. I graduated in June 1944 with my Pilot's wings and received my Second Lieutenant gold bars. Randolph Field, San Antonio, Texas came next for Twin Engine Instructors School. (Map 1.) and then back to Douglas, Arizona for a short period of advanced twin engine flight training.

When I received my orders to go overseas as a Commissioned Officer, I was sent back to Kearns Field, Utah for physical jungle survival training. Traveling by train I arrived at Camp Stoneman, at Pittsburg, California, for a final checkup on clothing and equipment, then boarded the USS *Catalina* that had been commandeered for war service. I rode it down the Sacramento River from Pittsburg to San Francisco on my way to a troop ship docked at Fisherman's Wharf in San Francisco. There, along with thousands of other military personnel, we boarded USS *General R.E. Callon.* As we sailed out of San Francisco Bay, I took a last look and waved goodbye to the Golden Gate Bridge, close to the hospital where I was born. At that moment I thought that I would probably not return from this terrible world war. As did so many other Americans of that era, I felt it was my patriotic duty to do my part in fighting the Japanese because of their sneak attack on Pearl Harbor.

Beverly
Christiansen

Beverly: My parents were pioneers. My mother Billie grew up on a farm in Alberta, Canada, along with three brothers and five sisters. She was adventuresome, especially for that time and her age, and managed to talk her father into letting her take the train to California to visit her married sister. There she met Lars Eariel Christiansen, the man who would eventually become my father. They married in Los Angeles, honeymooned in Avalon, Catalina Island, and lived in southern California where Chris had a succession of odd jobs, working in construction and as an extra in cowboy movies. His family had farms in Downy, Idaho and Cardston, Alberta, just across the border from Montana, the latter not far from her family home. When Billie found herself pregnant, she felt homesick for her family, so she and Chris moved to his old farm house in Cardston to await the baby. As fate would have it, when the baby started to come, their car broke down on the rough road to town in the midst of a storm. Her husband Chris half walked, half carried her back to the Cardston farmhouse where she gave birth to a premature baby boy. She survived, but the baby did not.

Fifteen months later, when my mother became pregnant again, she and Chris moved into town well in advance of her due date. I was born on April 4, 1928. Upon first seeing the new baby, my mother Billie said that she knew that the baby girl was born to make life an adventure. As a young girl, my mother had read George B. McCutcheon's book *Beverly of Graustark,* about an adventuresome young American girl, so Beverly became my name. When I was not yet a year old my parents began to plan their return to California, which was once again interrupted when they learned that my mother was pregnant. Once more California would have to wait. On September 28, 1930 another baby girl joined the family. They named my sister Avalon, after the small town on Catalina Island where they had honeymooned. My Dad also had a sense of adventure and when we made plans to go to California from Alberta, he decided to take a new highway that was under construction. It would shorten the route to the United States. It was not quite complete and there were sections where bridges had not been finished. Today it is highway 2 in Canada and highway 89 in Montana. The road went southwest into Montana over Logan Pass, straddling the Continental Divide and crossing the width of Glacier Park, down to Kalispell. Today it is called The Going-to-the-Sun road. At that time the road followed switchbacks straight down into a valley and where the road was incomplete, workmen had laid long split logs to connect the two sides of a crevice. To cross these places, my father got out of the car while my mother drove. He walked across the planks in front of the car, carrying a lantern, directing her so the wheels were lined up on the logs as we crossed over chasms with a deep drop below. I sat in the car, petrified, because my mother did not have a driver's license and as far as I knew, did not know how to drive. Somehow we made the journey without incident. To me, as young as I was, I've never forgot "The Road."

On the way south we discovered that my mother was pregnant again. This entailed another stop, this time at my grandfather's farm in Idaho where we waited for the baby to arrive. My next sister Carol was born on January 7, 1931. Once mom was ready to travel we continued our journey and ended up in the town of Indio, California. Dad had been able to find work on the new aqueduct project that brought water from the Colorado River to the Los Angeles Metropolitan Water District. Living in Indio was quite a change from the cold winters of Canada. When Dad was home on weekends we sometimes made trips to the Salton Sea to cool off. Also in Indio was where I first entered kindergarten. It took me four tries to find the right school. The closest school, right across the street from where we lived, turned out to be a Catholic school. Further up the street there was a boarding school for Indian kids and another for Spanish-speaking kids. Finally I found the public school and was admitted, even though I was too young for kindergarten. From the playground I noticed a small brown building on the other side of the playing field. Later I learned that that was a separate school for black children living in Indio.

During those years we moved every two years or so, as my Dad followed the progress of the aqueduct. Looking back, it seems curious, but we kids all enjoyed the moves. We liked the adventure of going someplace new. In those years following the depression we did not have much money; in fact, no one had much money. We would take vacations at places like Big Bear Lake, when my Dad could exchange work for rental of a mountain cabin. It was a time when people struggled to find jobs and make a living.

Living in Indio, when hobos or tramps would come to the door and ask to work for food, my mother would give them some small chore to do, such as chopping firewood or raking the yard, in return for a meal she served on the back porch. This was a family tradition that stemmed from my grandmother living on a farm in Idaho.

One time when I was four years old, I was sitting on the curb in front of our house eating a peanut butter sandwich. A young man whom I did not know came and sat down beside me. He told me how good my sandwich looked. Since my parents always fed anyone who came to our door, I offered to make him a sandwich.

He asked, "Do you have an onion?"

"Yes."

"Do you have any mustard?" I nodded yes again.

"Okay, if you would, slice the onion, put lots of mustard on the bread, and bring it out."

I went into the kitchen, set my sandwich on the counter, cut two slices of bread, and made the sandwich as directed. It looked so good that I made a second one for myself. I went back outside and we sat together eating our sandwiches. He thanked me and went on his way. I suppose you could say that times were different then. People were more trusting and trustworthy.

Dad had done well with the Metropolitan Water District and received several promotions. Once the project was completed he was placed in charge of the water system serving Los Angeles, Hollywood and the Beverly Hills area. We moved again, this time to the town of Highland

Park near Eagle Rock, where our house had a big yard with fruit trees and room for kids to play. There was the large eucalyptus tree that we could climb. We built a badminton court in the yard. We could take the streetcars to downtown Los Angeles or to the beach.

Dad had a company truck that he drove to work but we also had a big black Hupmobile sedan stored in a rented garage across the street. We used it when we went on trips. In 1939, when I was eleven years old, we took that car on a camping trip to Big Sur state park up in the redwoods. Dad cooked the food in a Dutch oven and over an open fire when we camped. There were a lot of people in the camp and in the evenings the Ranger would gather people for singing and other activities by a large bonfire. He came by our camp site and asked if anyone could sing, play an instrument, or dance, to be part of the evening's entertainment.

I didn't hesitate. I stepped up and said I would sing a song. The ranger started to write down my name on his clip board, but my mother interrupted.

"No, dear, let's let Carol sing." Although I was unaware of my short-coming, mother knew that I could not carry a tune, whereas my sister had a beautiful voice.

To our surprise, Carol shook her head, an adamant "no." She usually loved to be the center of attraction.

I had just turned eleven and being the oldest was quite confident. I planned to sing a song I'd heard over the new radio we'd recently acquired. It was sung by Kate Smith, and many times I'd sung it along with her, like we were a duet. Once again, I told the Ranger that I would sing a song, and he put my name on his list.

That afternoon I observed men and women standing around the cars that had radios. They were all intent on listening to the news. After the news ended, they stood in small groups discussing what they had heard. It seemed to be very important, but I was preoccupied with playing in the lake, practicing my song in my head, and paid no attention.

That evening we went to the camp center where there were flat logs for seats and a large stage. Below and in front of the stage there was a large bonfire. When my name was called, I marched myself up to the stage, and stood center front, took a hefty breath, and all alone began to belt out the song I'd sung with Kate Smith so often. With her voice accompanying me in my mind, the two of us sang her new hit song, "God Bless America."

When it was over, the entire audience stood and applauded me. My first and last public song and a standing ovation! I didn't understand the full import at the time, but on the radio the campers had learned that Hitler had marched into Poland and England had declared war on Germany. War was coming. Were we next? Everyone's mind was full of unanswerable questions. *God Bless America* was what everyone wanted to hear at that exact time. This day marked a new period in my life—in all our lives. We were dominated by thoughts of the war.

As the world moved closer to world war, I learned to live with rationing and scarcity. I got my first job at age 12 working in the Sweet Shop, a store that sold candy and ice cream. We all worked and found ways to get by. We had a victory garden at home. I had a sewing machine and made my own clothes. After graduating from high school, I went to work for the telephone company in Los Angeles. I had to take public transportation, the streetcar and buses, to get to my new job. It was time consuming, so I made a deposit with Ford Motor Company to pay for a new car so I could be independent. When the war was over they were going to start making automobiles again as soon as possible.

CHAPTER 2

EARNING MY WINGS

Bob: Thrilled at having passed the physical and the written exams for consideration to aviation training, the first time I ever had traveled outside of Southern California was when I was sent to Kearns Field Utah, as an army inductee for Basic Training. Following Kearns, I entered Denver University as an aviation cadet for some academic classes and besides studying hard, on campus as a cadet, we had a chance to ride and try our luck flying Piper Cubs (never solo) at a field near the campus, in the College Training Detachment there. I then reported to the Santa Ana Army Air Base (on what is now the Orange County Fair Grounds) for Pre Flight training; I was in Squadron 39. We never saw an airplane. This was essentially more Basic Training: march, march, march. Then run, run, run. Then march, march, march some more, in between, do pushups, pushups, pushups. This preparation led up to the various tests to determine if my skills were a match for pilot, navigator, or bombardier. It took a full week for both physical and mental tests. The examiners grilled me with questions to determine mental stability and sexual orientation. Physical stability was tested also, for example, how long I could hold a small rod centered in a ring, without touching the edge. As I concentrated on holding it steady, they would make a loud noise by my ear, to startle me. These were all tests to determine who could be qualified as a pilot, navigator, or bombardier. Pilot was always in my mind. When I was finally chosen as a potential pilot, after the months of training it was the best news ever.

By this time I had turned 19, but everything was still an adventure, so on to Wickenburg Arizona, for Primary Training. I soloed in a

PT-17 Stearman Biplane. I was flying in the rear seat, instructor in front seat, both with open cockpits. He was making me fly "touch and go's," that is where one lands without stopping, and just keeps rolling to take right off again. After doing this a number of times the instructor asked me to stop on the next landing. He got out and said, "Okay, go do it on your own." That was my solo flight. During training flights I learned how to fly in formation, perform all kinds of acrobatics and make good landings. We always wore a parachute ready to bail out if we had a major problem.

When doing spins we were trained to bail out if we could not recover from a spin at a given altitude. Thankfully, I always was able to recover. I also used a seat pack parachute because with my shorter height it gave me a more comfortable flying position to look for other flying aircraft.

Bob in Cockpit of a Basic Trainer

Visual observation of the sky was very important to avoid other training aircraft.

During time off we caught a ride into town to visit with local females and take in a movie. The movie theatre was such that wewe had to sit on orange crates and bring our own snacks. I recall spending Christmas

1943 in Prescott Arizona, high in the mountains. It was snowing in town but warm and cozy in the Hacienda Hotel located just off the town square. The hotel personnel and the local population took good care of us. This was my very first Christmas away from home.

Sent to Minter Field in Bakersfield California for basic flight training, we flew BT-13s, nicknamed the "Vultee Vibrator." It was an all metal, low wing, single engine trainer capable of performing violent acrobatics. I enjoyed doing acrobatics, they were fun. At this station there was limited time off which we pilots mostly spent in Bakersfield bars and dance halls.

Moving on from Bakersfield I went to Douglas Arizona for Advanced Flight School and learned how to fly the AT-17, twin engine type aircraft. that were called "Bamboo Bombers" because they were made of wood stringers that were covered in fabric. Here we learned how to navigate, fly in close formation and on instruments only. During leisure time many of us traveled across the border to Agua Prieta, Mexico where we were warmly accepted by the population and shopped for presents to send home.

I earned my wings in Douglas Arizona on June 27, 1944. At the time I was an enlisted cadet. First I signed my honorable discharge papers as an enlisted man. It was dated June 26th. For a few seconds I was out of the service, but in a few more seconds they made me sign on as a commissioned 2nd Lieutenant, and presented me with my wings. This was a wonderful day for me. I graduated in a class called 44f. Translated, 44 meant 1944, and f, the sixth letter of the alphabet, stood for June, the sixth month. After receiving our wings and commissions the tradition was to give the first enlisted man that saluted us as we walked by a dollar, so the crew chiefs were all standing in a line as we walked out of the commissioning ceremony with our gold bars. Some of them saluted more than 100 times.

While at Douglas, on a routine training flight, we were scheduled to take off in the morning as a flight of three AT-17s, each with a pilot and copilot. Our mission was to rendezvous at 10,000 feet and practice close formation flying. Initially I was the right wingman in the vee-formation. After an hour or so of flying, with the hot desert air thermals bouncing the planes around, my right engine started losing power so I swerved away from the formation. I called the tower and told them we had a problem and were returning. Meanwhile, my copilot, airman Moskowitz, and I worked frantically with the fuel valves and a wobble pump to try to get the engine running right. About that time the other engine started sputtering also. We were about fifteen miles out but the tower cleared the field for our approach. I thought we could make it but at about 3 miles out both engines quit and I knew we were not going to make the field. I called the tower again and advised that we were not going to make it; we were going to land in the desert. The procedure called for a wheels up, belly landing, to avoid flipping the plane. Though this was done successfully, I have vivid memories of dirt and bits of cactus flying by the windshield as the plane ground its way into the desert soil before slowly coming to a halt. My copilot banged his head on the instrument panel but other than that we both walked away from the plane, which was demolished. This was crash number one for me. It was later determined that the cause of the engine failure was vapor lock in

AT-17 Forced Landing, Douglas Arizona

the fuel lines caused by excessive desert heat.[2] The second one occurred months later in the Philippines and had the potential to be much more serious. That time, the plane was carrying two 2000 pound bombs as cargo. More about that later.

From Douglas I was sent to Randolph Field, Texas to attend twin-engine instructor's school. Pilots were scarce, so new ones were made instructors right away to gain flying hours. After just a few weeks there I returned to Douglas Arizona now as an instructor to train cadets for a few more weeks before I was sent back to Kearns Field Utah to do combat training for overseas duty. Near the end of September, 1944 I was ordered to report to San Francisco for transport overseas. On September 25, 1944 I boarded the troop ship USS *General R. E. Callon* for the long cruise to the South Pacific, destination New Guinea, where I would become part of the 5th Air Force. I had just turned 20 years old, and about to embark on a new phase of my life.

Large WWII Era Radio Dominates Room against Wall, Beverly on R.

The Three Sisters Learn to use Guns

CHAPTER 3

THE HOME FRONT

Beverly: When people were finally all tuned in to the reality of war, it was the beginning of a different life for all of us at the home front. Soon supplying the growing Armed Forces and our frontline allies across the Atlantic with essential materials caused shortages at home. Shipping was allocated to sending important things abroad and stopped bringing us many things, such as bananas, that we had grown used to. Rationing became a reality. My parents had to stand in lines to get ration books that were filled with little coupons indicating when and how much we could buy of a given product such as sugar, butter, or coffee. Many nonfood items were also rationed, such as gasoline and leather goods. Production of new cars stopped. Canvas shoes, like tennis shoes, were available, but we girls did not like them. Instead we wore flats, penny loafers, and sandals, all without socks. Silk Stockings were not available, but we used a brown eyebrow pencil to a draw a line from our heel to above the knee, giving the appearance of a seam on the back of those long sheer stockings that were no longer available.

On Sunday morning, December 7, 1941 reality grew closer. While sitting on the floor of our living room, Avalon, Carol, and I did what we always did at that time on a Sunday in December. We finished reading the funny papers and began to page through the colorful ads describing Christmas toys, trying to decide what we wanted Santa Claus to bring us. The radio was on and suddenly my parents jumped closer to it when the announcer began excitedly telling the world about the Japanese sneak attack on Pearl Harbor. Like a puff of smoke, Santa

Claus disappeared from our thoughts as it seemed to us that we would all be bombed and dead before Christmas. We had seen the magazine pictures and the newsreels at the Saturday movies of terrible battles and bombings in Europe. It was frightening to think that this danger might reach California.

Our parents tried to reassure us by explaining how far away Hawaii was. But the radio announcer asked the question "Was California next? Had the Japanese bombed our fleet in Hawaii, to prepare for invading the U.S. mainland and California next?" He went on to say that in effect, California was cut off from the rest of the United States by the Rocky Mountains, and there was only limited access to the West Coast. "We had better get prepared to defend ourselves" was his final comment.

With the advent of the war my Dad now carried two guns, a rifle hanging in the rear window of the truck and a handgun. These were necessary to defend the water supplies if on his rounds he found anyone trying to sabotage our water. We girls were made familiar with the guns and even taken out in the desert to shoot them. My youngest sister Carol liked this but I did not. Our parents were careful to explain the dangers of the guns and to make sure that we knew enough not to play with them. This was driven home one night when, after we were in bed, Dad got out the guns to clean them and accidentally shot a hole in our piano. The hole is there today, left as a permanent reminder of the danger of "unloaded" guns.

While the West Coast was somewhat cut off from the rest of the country, here we had the resources and the people, plus a will to mobilize. Soon the southern half of the West Coast was rapidly producing aircraft while the northern half built ships. It was almost as if we became a country of our own, on our own, succeeding beyond expectation. With the food shortage and rationing, Dad converted our whole back yard except for the badminton court into a garden. We grew tomatoes, green beans, zucchini, and other produce. He

Victory Garden, Peas and Chickens

raised bees for honey. The chicken coop was repaired and filled with chickens and rabbits, so we had eggs and meat, even if it wasn't steaks.

We were still living in Highland Park when I started junior high school. Not far from where we lived there were two very large public swimming pools that we could walk to for a swim on hot summer days. One was the Eagle Rock plunge, which charged five cents for a towel and a key to a locker. We would swim until noon and then go to a nearby park and eat our lunch. The other option was the Highland Park pool which was a little bit further away from our house. One day we went on a Wednesday and found the pool to be closed, even though it was full of kids.

When I ask why, the attendant told me "That Wednesdays were reserved for colored children."

"But why?" I asked, "why do they get a day all to themselves?"

"Because they are not allowed in on any other day, just Wednesdays," was the answer.

At the time, I did not really understand this answer. As we three girls walked home, we agreed that these kids should be able to come any day they wanted to, and we should be able to also. All these attitudes changed after the war ended, slowly at first, but then more rapidly as the old barriers came down.

Civil defense began to be practiced in each community and taught in the schools. We practiced for an air raid at school. Everyone had a task to do. Some stood on the roof to watch for planes. The older boys were given a pail of sand and a shovel to be ready to put on any incendiary bombs that might be dropped from a plane to start fires. Girls were sent to the gym to take care of injured. We were shown charts that had black silhouettes of Japanese planes, so we would know one if we saw it. At night adult men and women stayed up to watch for these planes and sound the warning. Air raid sirens were periodically tested so we would know what to do if we heard one blowing. The men who served as air raid wardens in each neighborhood walked about at night to see if anyone had a light showing around their newly placed blackout curtains. Every light had to be off or not showing, so the bombers would not know where people and buildings were located. Everyone was supposed to go inside at the sound of a siren, however my friends and I rushed to a neighbor's house that was on the highest hill, where we could look out towards the ocean and see the searchlights combing the sky and lighting up the small blimps that were tethered along the shore to prevent planes from coming in low.

Just across the street from the school was a short block lined with stores. The most important one to me was called the Sweet Shop. It sold candy and large ice cream cones for a nickel. This store had a huge impact on my life. My best friend, DeLayne, (nicknamed Dee) and I decided that we wanted to try to get a job at the Sweet Shop. It was on our way to every place we went, school, Saturday movies, the public swimming pool, and downtown Highland Park, so we always stopped there to buy five cents worth of candy to last us through the day for any event we attended. The store owner, Mrs. Brownly made all the candy and chocolates by hand herself.

One day Dee and I went in and spoke with a man, who turned out to be Mr. Brownly. He asked how old we were. I was twelve, but Dee was only eleven. He was kind to us and explained that we had to have work permits, and you had to be twelve years old to get them. That left out Dee. We said we'd be back when Dee was twelve and we had work permits.

When Dee was twelve years old we got our work permits and returned to the store. The man was not there. We spoke with Mrs. Brownly, who told us that she didn't have an opening at that time. I told her that we talked to a man, and he said that when we got work permits, we could have a job. She asked us to describe the man. When we did, she changed her mind and said that maybe she could hire one of us. Initially she was reluctant to hire two girls, but when we said we'd split the twenty-five cents an hour salary she was offering for one person, she agreed. Later we learned that the man we'd met was her husband, and he'd passed away.

Soon we demonstrated our worth and she paid us each twenty-five cents per hour. Having us in the store actually turned out to be a great help for her, because she could work in the back making candy and not be interrupted every time a customer came in. I learned a lot of important life lessons working in the Sweet Shop, lessons that helped me later on. I felt comfortable meeting new people and talking to them. This experience ultimately helped me in other jobs I had as I grew older.

One day while working I heard planes approaching overhead. I rushed from the counter and looked out the door. It was a formation of six P-38 Lightnings, my favorite plane. For some reason I just loved their distinctive twin body design. They were built by Lockheed Aircraft Corporation in nearby Burbank, California. A customer who had been sitting at the counter followed me outside to look.

P-38

"Aren't they breathtaking," I said.

"They sure are," he said, before returning to the counter.

A few weeks later the same customer came into the store and placed a tiny box on the counter. "For you," he said.

After some initial hesitation on my part (I'd been taught not to accept gifts from strangers), he tipped the box open to display a tiny golden P-38 charm on a matching chain. Apparently he worked at Lockheed and had picked it up there. To overcome my hesitation, he left it as a "tip." At the time, little did I know how significant that airplane would be to the war effort. It served in Europe, but in the Pacific was where it played a key role. A year or so after I received the P-38 charm, American intelligence learned that Admiral Yamamoto, the architect of the Pearl Harbor attack, was flying to Bougainville Island to inspect Japanese forces. A flight of sixteen P-38s was dispatched from Guadalcanal to intercept his plane. Although it was at an extreme distance, they found the Japanese planes—two bombers and an escort of six fighters—and shot down the bombers and several of the fighters. Afterwards, neither side could mention the incident. The Americans could not say anything, because it would reveal that they had broken the Japanese code. The Japanese could not reveal that Yamamoto was dead, because it would have been a huge blow to morale. Of course, we didn't know any of this until after the war ended.

Rationing had an effect on the Sweet Shop as well. We couldn't get bananas so the banana split dishes were put away until after the war ended. Sugar and cream shortages required us to sell more sherbet and less ice cream. We had to figure out ways to make our customers happy with that change.

People in the war industries came to our school and asked us for help making gloves, picking fruit, doing other chores to support the war effort. We collected grease, scrap metal, and newspapers. I was able to get some other jobs in addition to working in the Sweet Shop. One was with a large department store and another was at the United Artists Theater down in Los Angeles. As the war progressed schools initiated a four-four plan. Kids who had jobs could go to school for four hours and then leave for four hours of work. Among other things, my Dad bought me a sewing machine so I could make my own clothes.

We had lots of other experiences trying to do our part in the war effort. Mrs. Brownly had a son named Mike, who helped in the Sweet Shop when not in school. He wanted to join the Navy but had gotten an exemption because his mother was a widow and he had to help support her. Mike was like a big brother to Dee and me. One day he asked me if I would write letters to a friend of his named Conrad who was serving in the South Pacific. At first I hesitated, "I don't even know the guy," I said.

Beverly Age 14

"That's not important, Mike said. "He's in the Pacific fighting Japs. Just getting mail will mean a lot to him."

As Mike requested, I wrote to Conrad. I had my Dad take some pictures of me to send to him. Dad seemed to know what the guys would like. We exchanged quite a few letters, but sadly he was killed, along with thousands more of our men, in the invasion of Okinawa. Mike and I were both very saddened by Conrad's death.

This brought the war much closer, more personal. One day, much later, Conrad's mother, whom I also had never met, wrote to me to thank me for writing to her son. He had written to her, telling her that my letters had made his days happier.

Around the time it came for me to graduate from high school, the Metropolitan Water District decided to move my Dad to a pumping station on top of Mulholland Drive, on the border between Hollywood and Beverly Hills. This critical facility needed 24-hour a day monitoring. The company purchased a house that sat nearby on Oakshire Drive and we shortly moved in to this new home. After I graduated, the job in the department store went away and I began to look for other work. I really needed to earn enough money to buy a car once they started becoming available again, as it was difficult to commute from our new home to any place where I could work. I had to take a bus and then the streetcars to get down town. I heard about job openings at the telephone company and so went down to the office and applied. I was accepted and given a job in an office on Vermont Boulevard, where I made friends with a pretty blonde girl named Mary Mosier. We spent our free time together shopping on Hollywood Boulevard or going out for lunch at local places. My friendship with Mary led to the biggest and most profound change in my entire life. The war had ended and her two brothers were coming home from the Army Air Force. The eldest brother Jack was coming home

Bob's Sister, Mary Mosier

from Texas with his bride. The younger one, Bob, was single and was a pilot returning from the South Pacific. Mary had a clipboard with Bob's picture on it and she was canvassing girls working on the switchboards to line up some dates for Bob when he returned. I could see he was good looking and had a nice smile. She asked me, but "signing up" didn't appeal to me. I didn't want my name on a list of girls, so I said no thanks.

PART II

- **NEW GUINEA BY TROOP SHIP** • **JOIN THE 57ᵀᴴ TCS**
- **MOVE TO BIAK ISLAND** • **MISSIONS IN SOUTHWEST PACIFIC**
- **PARATROOP DROPS** • **GLIDER TOWS** •**CAPTURE OF PELELIU.**

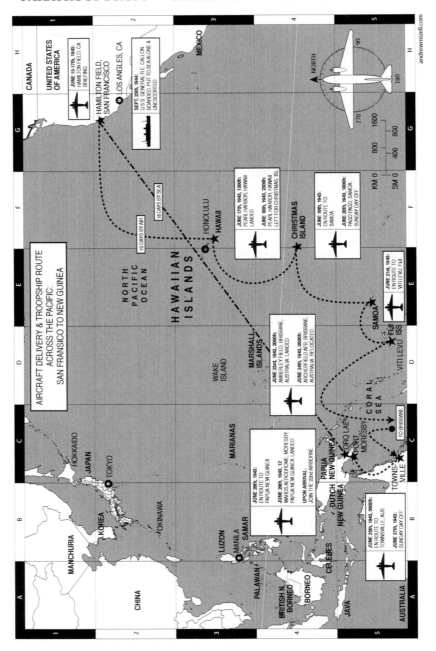

CHAPTER 4

ON TO NEW GUINEA

Bob: I was on the USS *General R.E. Callon,* AP-139, for 18 days. She was a new troop ship, built by Kaiser in Richmond, California, and commissioned in August, 1944. This was either her first or second voyage. We did not see any land,

not Hawaii, none of the Pacific islands, but kept a careful lookout for Japanese submarines. I did not like being in a rolling ship. I had trouble sleeping. As an Officer we had good accommodations but it didn't help me. To sleep, I would play poker in the Officer's Mess for hours on end, sometimes for 48 hours straight except for food breaks, until I was so tired I then would be able to sleep. After a night, I would repeat the process. If you have to travel by troop ship make sure you are a commis-

USS *General R.E. Callon Troopship* sioned officer. My quarters were nice, a bunk bed, clean sheets, pillow, porthole for air. In spite of all that, I could not get to sleep.

On the troopship, I had a lot of time to think about where I was going and why. From the newspapers we knew that in the five months following Pearl Harbor, Imperial Japanese forces had an unbroken string of victories that enable them to capture critical bases as far south as the Solomon Islands, including Guadalcanal Island. To put this in perspective,

Guadalcanal was south of the equator and over 11,500 statute miles from Tokyo. In comparison, Los Angeles was only slightly more than 6,900 miles from Tokyo. If those of us living on the West Coast needed any reason to be concerned about Japanese intentions, the Japanese attack on Pearl Harbor certainly left us feeling vulnerable.

In April 1942 the Japanese high command developed a plan for capturing Port Moresby, New Guinea. (Full details of this operation, which was called "Plan MO," were not known until after the war.) At the time about all we knew was that the Japanese were threatening Australia. With control of this vital port and its airfields, Japan could attack Australia and cut off Allied approaches to Japanese bases in the Southwest Pacific. Our intelligence discovered the Japanese were moving troops and resources south, so two U.S. carrier task forces were sent into the South Pacific to attack the Japanese. In May 1942 the Battle of the Coral Sea took place. Sometimes called a draw since there was no clear victor, in reality the Battle of the Coral Sea was a setback for the Japanese. The invasion of Port Moresby was canceled. Finally, the southward march of the Imperial Japanese Army had been stopped. Later, they would try to take Port Moresby by land, crossing over the treacherous Owen Stanley mountain range where the jungle would extract a terrible toll on the Japanese soldiers. This too would end in failure.

A month later in June 1942, near a small island called Midway, the Japanese Navy suffered a huge defeat with the sinking of four fleet carriers.

In August 1942 Allied forces invaded Guadalcanal and over the next six months successfully repulsed multiple Japanese efforts to recapture Henderson airfield. Japan attempted to reinforce the island with troops brought in by destroyers at night, or carried in on submarines and barges, all with limited success. They were attacked repeatedly by Allied air power and naval forces. Desperate for food, ammunition, and medicine, the Japanese even tried to float in supplies in empty oil drums.

Meanwhile, in October 1942, C-47 Troop Carriers transported an entire battalion of Australian troops to the Wanigela airstrip in the Tufi Peninsula, located in the New Guinea jungle. On the first day, 60 planes landed and unloaded their cargo in an average of seven minutes. In January 1943, when the Japanese tried to capture Wau, again in New Guinea, the defending Australian forces were quickly reinforced and resupplied by air. Over a critical four days, 244 separate C-47 landings were made and unloaded under enemy fire. The Wau strip, 3,300 feet long, was unusual in that one end is about 300 feet higher than the other end. Early in the New Guinea campaign air mobility had proved its worth.

In December 1942 the Imperial Army high command made the decision to withdraw from Guadalcanal. In January and February 1943 the Japanese succeeded in withdrawing over 10,000 men from the island.

There was a clear lesson to be learned from Guadalcanal. In the far reaches of the Pacific, victory went to the side that could deliver the most troops and supplies the quickest. The U.S. rushed the development of a new type of airplane—unarmed C-47 troop carrier transports that could rapidly bring in soldiers and military supplies and were capable of landing on crude jungle air strips. The motto of the Troop Carrier Command was *"Vincit Qui Primum Gerit,"* which meant "He conquers who gets there first."

In the succeeding months of 1943 the Allies continued their relentless push north. In March 1943 they drove to Bougainville Island and also captured the Gilbert Islands. By April 1944 they had retaken Hollandia with its important harbor and airfields. Next Wakde Island was captured, and then Biak Island in August 1944. These efforts were aided by C-47 troop carriers flying from airfields at Nadzab or Hollandia. By September 1944 all of New Guinea was under Allied control except for isolated Japanese units cut off from any source of supply and struggling to avoid starvation.

The long march back to Tokyo had begun in earnest. It was at this point that I joined the war.

On the ship, I was assigned to keep the enlisted troops from shooting craps and raising hell in the decks below. They were packed in—sleeping 4 high in hammocks and were not happy being cooped up in the bowels of the ship. I can't say I blamed them. I carried a 45 caliber automatic as a side arm so I could protect myself, but it would not have been much help. Those troops were big, mean, and on edge. When I found them in the quarters playing craps and cards I was supposed to stop them. No way. I stayed friendly and tried to ignore their actions and keep myself from getting killed. If they attacked I would never be found, four decks down, full of humanity, sweating in the tropic heat. I thought it best not to make them mad.

As we passed over the equator around the Gilbert Islands, the "Ancient Order of the Deep" took over the ship. All the "old salts" on board took advantage of hazing the troops (newbies), however all the Commissioned Officers had a more reserved ceremony. They just cut our hair, painted us all colors that didn't wash off, brought us before the court of King Neptune and dunked us. This initiation gave the participants a life-long membership in the "Ancient Order of the Deep." So the next time you crossed the equator, you were in command to define the initiation for the new first timers—and it goes on and on. (Flying over the equator at 10,000 feet does not qualify one for being initiated into the "Ancient Order of the Deep.")

In the South Pacific as we steamed through the Bismarck Archipelago and Solomon Islands we had glimpses of very dense green jungles and tall trees, split apart by a landing strips carved by the Navy Seabees (CBs, or Construction Battalions).

The landing strips were either graded coral, glaring white against the deep green jungle, or soft ground that was covered by heavy dark metal landing mats. Known formally as "Marston Matting," these were pierced steel planks, pieces of steel with perforated holes to reduce the weight without taking away the strength needed to keep our heavy aircraft from sinking into the mud.

Our South Pacific destination was Oro Bay and Langemak Bay, Papua New Guinea Territory. After 18 days of no sleep and continuous poker games we arrived.

We were joining the 57th Troop Carrier Squadron—nicknamed "The Biscuit Bombers"—that had first arrived in New Guinea on June 28,

1943. The first thirteen C-47s of our squadron had been flown from the central United States to Hamilton Field, near Novato, California and then to New Guinea, a distance of over 11,500 miles. The pilots were briefed on communications and procedures for ditching at sea. Each plane had a crew of five: pilot, co-pilot, navigator, crew chief, and radio operator. With no cargo on board the C-47 maximum range was extended. The first leg was Hamilton to Honolulu, slightly more than 2,300 miles. The planes left at dawn and arrived in Honolulu at 3:00 PM. After refueling and an 8 hour layover, they took off and flew the next leg to Christmas Island (now called Kiritimati) in the Gilbert Island group. The next stops were American Samoa, then Viti Levu in the Fiji Group, New Caledonia, and finally Brisbane Australia. Then they flew north along the Australian coast to Townsville and across the Coral Sea to Port Moresby. The ground echelon of several hundred officers and enlisted men departed Camp Stoneman, were transported to San Francisco and on June 27, 1943, boarded the *SS Lurline* troopship for the long voyage to Australia and thence to New Guinea. Now, one year later, I was on my way to join those who had blazed the way. The pilots of the 57th with most seniority were anxious to have replacements so they could go home.

When our ship pulled into port, there were Army ground troops waiting to get on board for their trip back to the U.S. They had put in their tour of duty fighting the Japanese in the New Guinea jungle. Many of them were wounded. We were green troops arriving to replace them. As they came on board ship they told us about what we were getting into—one horror story after another. They told me that as soon as we stepped off the boat and went into the jungle we would be ambushed by Japanese that were hiding up in the trees. All my pilot buddies and I were really worried about getting off with all our gear on our backs and walking into the jungle. We took the ride to shore in a landing craft and as we stepped off onto the sandy beach we were expecting the worst. We were greeted by trucks from our assigned squadron. The truck driver told us to be careful and keep our eyes open for trouble. He then headed down a narrow dirt road into the jungle. We were extremely anxious about what might happen next. Along the road there were many tent cities with thousands of Army troops and supply depots stacked high with provisions.

As we drove on the winding road, with thick solid jungle on both sides, we were amazed by the tremendous amounts of supplies lined up along open spaces in the road. Later we found out that if you had a bottle of booze you could bargain for anything in the supply depot. For a fifth of whisky you could trade for a Jeep, or a refrigerator, or whatever. Unfortunately, none of us had any booze until later, after we took combat leave in Sydney, Australia. We did not see a single Japanese soldier along the way.

New Guinea Native

What we did see were "Fuzzy Wuzzies." Fuzzy Wuzzy was a generic name given by Australian troops to any of indigenous peoples of Papuan New Guinea. The name was derived from the frizzy hair style of the natives. During the fighting with the Japanese, they aided the Allies and rescued many wounded soldiers. The males we observed were the heads of a family and typically had several wives and a few kids. Fuzzy Wuzzies lived in a cleared space in the jungle with grass huts spaced around in a circle with the center open for common activities. As the man walked down the road with his family he carried a long spear and wore a loin cloth, and nothing else. The man walked down the road with his head high. His wives followed behind about 10 paces and carried all their belongings. The women following him had their possessions on their backs, heads, and arms, so loaded down that they could hardly walk. We were told that he must be ready at all times to protect his family from harm.

As the truck bumped along on the muddy road into more and more dense jungle with less and less troop camps, it started to look like we were now getting into scary jungle warfare areas that we had seen in many war propaganda movies. Don't forget that we just got off the boat and left civilization behind for the first time in our (mostly) young lives. We now had nothing except what we were able to carry on our backs. I kept feeling to see if my Army 45 caliber side arm was still in my reach and ready to go.

We kept bouncing down the narrow dirt road not knowing what to expect next. We were looking all around especially up in the jungle treetop canopy, wondering if what we were told would all of a sudden be real. We soon came upon an open space in the jungle that was obviously a landing strip with steel landing mat. The truck drove on down to the end of the runway, past a number of C-47 cargo planes and P-47 fighter aircraft and then we saw our sign "5TH AIRFORCE, 57TH SQUAD-RON" with a logo that later was called the "Tokyo Trolley." The Tokyo Trolley looked like a cartoon of the San Francisco cable cars. We were at Nadzab, New Guinea. The Lae and Nadzab airfield areas had been recently captured by American and Australian Forces. The airfield was taken when hundreds of paratroopers were dropped from C-47s early in September, 1944.

We drove through the squadron gate and saw how we were going to live for the next few years. There was a tent for squadron headquarters, another for a mess hall, and rows of tents disappearing into the jungle. We were greeted by the Operations Officer with a big smile as he said "Welcome to the 5th Air Force, we have been waiting for you as our replacements for months, glad you are here." So we now set up our own tents and cots using 10-in-1 ration wood crates for a dresser. Each one of us also had a footlocker that came in a separate truck. We spent a couple of days getting indoctrinated into the squadron. The food was mostly from rations that were conditioned to last in the tropical jungle heat, which made them taste like nothing you ever tasted. The 10-in-1 rations were the best. The mess hall food was acceptable if you liked creamed, chipped beef on toast (known affectionately as SOS or "shit on a shingle"), or spam and powdered milk and powdered eggs.

We were eager to start our flight training in the C-47's. The 375th Troop Carrier Group consisted of Troop Carrier Squadrons 55, 56, 57, and 58. We received orders to move north to Biak Island in Dutch New Guinea, at the opposite end from Port Moresby. We loaded up the whole

Bob and Other 57th Squadron Pilots
(Standing L to R) 2nd Lt Thomas R. Klomparens, 2nd Lt. Craig D. Headley,
2nd Lt. Robert Mosier, 2nd Lt. Russel R. Kibbe, Jr.
(seated L to R) 2nd Lt Morton Mantell, 2nd Lt Miroslav C. Parma.

squadron into 21 C-47's and flew to Biak. After making several trips and waiting several days for the ships to arrive at Biak with more of our gear, we started our training.[3] I was assigned to Troop Carrier Squadron 57, flying as a copilot.

After I had become proficient in flying the C-47 (a militarized version of the DC-3, officially called the Skytrain, but also known as the Gooney Bird in the Navy and the Dakota in England), I earned my 1st Pilot rating in that aircraft. Proficiency was determined by the fact that the squadron was short of 1st Pilots, because they were either on front line flight missions, or ready to return home to the good old U.S.A., or on combat R&R (rest and recuperation) leave in Sydney Australia. When supplies were needed by the front line ground forces, new 1st pilots would be selected from the group of copilots that were in training or in their tents catching up on sleep. The copilot with the most copilot air time would be selected on the spot and promoted to 1st pilot and immediately sent out to the flight line with another copilot to fly personnel and cargo to where it was needed on the front lines. Most of the new copilots were 19 or 20 years old. I was 20 years old

10 in 1 Rations

and was willing to fly anywhere through any type of weather any time day or night. I just loved to fly.

With that twisted sense of humor that existed in wartime, because we dropped food and supplies to the troops, rather than bombs, our squadron 57 aircraft became known unofficially as "The Biscuit Bombers."

"Biscuit Bombers" Drop Crates of Supplies

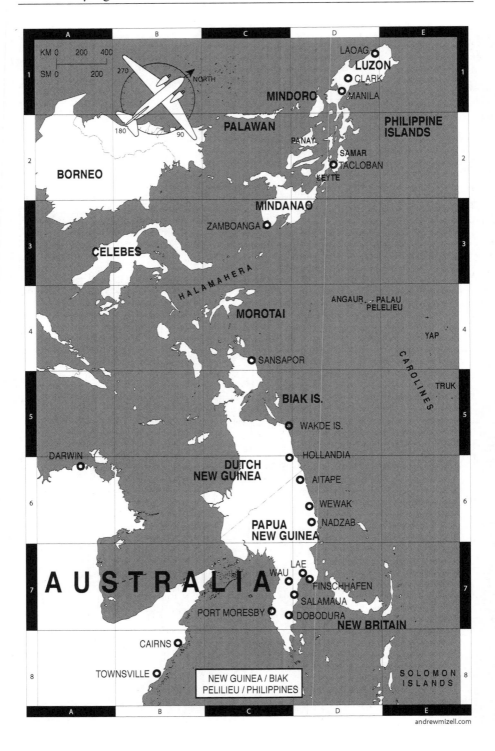

CHAPTER 5

MOVE TO BIAK

I joined the squadron in New Guinea in 1944, and after a month or so moved to Biak Island. I was stationed on Biak for approximately six months. We were a Troop Carrier Group located on a landing strip that was shared with a B-24 Bomber Group and a field hospital with a few female Army nurses. After only about 4 hours of air time and about 8 hours of ground school we were checked out as C-47 copilots, thus becoming official members of the Squadron. Before long we were flying cargo and passengers all over New Guinea and associated islands.

The Island of Biak was 45 miles long and 23 miles wide, or about the size of Maui, Hawaii. It had a flat area in the southern part that was developed by the Marines and Seabees as a forward area airstrip for our Troop Carrier Wing (The 55th, 56th, 57th, and 58th Troop Carrier Squadrons) and a B-24 Bomber Group. Biak is located in a large Dutch New Guinea (Indonesia) Bay. It is one of the Schouten Islands. New Guinea is the second largest island in the world, ranking just behind Greenland. New Guinea essentially surrounds one side of Biak and the other side looks out to the North, toward the Peleliu Islands, with nothing in sight except the South Pacific Ocean. Biak Island is located one degree south of the equator. Biak and New Guinea are essentially tropical rain forests with an average 200 inches of rain per year. (See map 3).

Four pilots were assigned to a specific tent, usually alphabetically by last name. Each of us had a cot and blankets, but no pillow. Our cots were foldable canvas that also could be used for sleeping under our aircraft when staying overnight on a mission. We used old wooden crates for tables to write on and hold our sundries. We put the crates together in the center when we played cards or craps. You could bargain with others and get things to make you more comfortable if you had the right bargaining chips. You could get almost anything you wanted if you had a bottle of rum or any other type of drinkable alcohol, or you could use cash on payday. For meals, we walked to the mess hall three times a day. When on a mission, we walked to the Operations tent for mission briefings. We had to walk into the jungle to use the latrine. We had very little leisure time. It was also very dangerous to do a lot of sightseeing in the jungle or to search the caves along the sea cliffs. Fishing or swimming close to the squadron base was acceptable. If an aircraft was available on one of our free days, we could schedule it for a training flight and fly around the island sightseeing above the jungle and seeing where the natives lived in remote areas and how they set up their villages. Sometimes we would skim above the jungle treetops and wing wave at them.

We had a few things to read, mostly army issued regulations and technical manuals and a few comic books. However, most sought after were several sexually-oriented romantic novels and stories passed from flier to flier. They were brought back by pilots that had enough combat time to get 10 days of rest and recuperation (R&R) in Sydney Australia. The X-rated books were good bargaining items and were usually pretty worn out after they'd made the rounds of multiple readers.

Early in the morning on a mission day we would use a Jeep to get to our assigned aircraft on the flight line. We each carried our flight plans and seat pack parachutes. We relied on the Crew Chief and assigned ground crew for that aircraft to get it ready for the day's mission. If we were lucky, the Crew Chief would stock it with the best rations for the flight. Note: To understand what it was like to fly a transport aircraft in 1944 compared to today, see the Appendix.

The Squadron had around 23 to 25 flyable C-47s and later there were both C-47s and C-46s. Operations matched up pilots and crews for each mission. We usually took off at 5:00 A.M. to have plenty of

Capt. Pennock in Intelligence Briefing Pilots.
Bob in cap, foreground

daylight to find our remote island destination. Each pilot usually had a different aircraft assigned to him for each mission, so after a period of time we had a chance to learn the flying characteristics of each aircraft. We eventually learned that certain aircraft were unbalanced and some flew better than others. Each had their own personalities. We kept busy figuring out with our cargo load the best airspeed, fuel consumption and a dozen other parameters to properly estimate our route and time of arrival within our fuel range for our specific mission.

Our duties were to fly supplies and personnel quickly to where they were most urgently needed. In the evening we would play poker in our tent waiting for our next day assignments. The assignments were scheduled by the Operations Officer. Flying a group of new nurse replacements from Nadzab New Guinea, when they arrived by troop hospital ships from the U.S., north to the Island of Biak was probably one of our best duties. The operations officer assigned these flights to the more senior 1st Pilots. So the copilots drew straws for this tough duty.

The nurses stayed isolated in their own quarters. If a nurse was interested in visiting our camp they could figure out a way and join us in groups for a nice evening discussion or sing along with a 10 to 1 ratio of men for each nurse that made it impossible for any hanky panky. In the air, on a mission, the ratio was reversed, especially when we were making a major camp relocation. It was always fun to show the nurses how to use the drift meter or shoot the stars from the overhead observation window. We were cautious about showing off the cockpit, because the Head nurse on-board always kept everyone in line. This area being a tropical rain forest, the humidity was always high and everything stayed wet. Our clothes and equipment would get moldy overnight. Every morning we would have to wipe off the green fungus from our boots. Leather was a natural for fungus. Fungus also grew in parts of your body, like in-between your toes. Personal hygiene was very important or you could easily get infections that we called the "Creeping Crud."

Malaria was very prevalent throughout the South Pacific. There was no drug protection against getting malaria. All we had during the war was a drug called Sulfa. Penicillin came later. Atabrine was a drug that only kept control of malaria symptoms but did not prevent the disease. We all had to take one Atabrine pill every morning. After several days of taking Atabrine, our skin turned yellow. I'm not kidding. It looked like we were getting a Japanese skin tint to use as a camouflage in the jungle. We all looked like we had yellow jaundice. I didn't lose my yellow glow until months after I stopped taking Atabrine. The pill was like a strong yellow dye. We would put one pill in a bucket of water and that one pill would contain enough yellow coloring to color all the T-shirts of our basketball team bright yellow.

We flew missions to the rear lines, south towards Australia, to places like Port Moresby, Lae, and Wewak to pick up supplies to take up to the front lines for our ground troops and bomber groups that were fighting (island hopping) their way north towards an invasion of the main Islands of Japan. When we landed at these remote landing strips hewed out of the New Guinea jungle we had to protect ourselves, because Japanese

C-47's Near New Guinea

snipers were always lurking nearby and taking pot shots at us. We lost several squadron members from sniper fire.

We tried to get in and get out fast. The Japanese would also launch concentrated mortar fire on the airstrip when they saw us land with our slow unarmed transport type aircraft. The only firepower we carried was our side arms, except that the aircraft usually had a Thompson sub-machine gun on board. Not always, because it was up to the Crew Chief, unless the 1st Pilot made a special request. We could grab the machine gun, and strafe the treetops only if we were in an isolated area. However the normal procedure was to call in fighter protection and ask them to strafe a certain area to stop Japanese attacks on our parked aircraft. I was lucky and didn't get a scratch, however it was very scary to see the dense jungle only a few feet away and not know whether or not there were Japanese snipers lurking nearby or getting ready for a charge. They were very fanatical and willing to commit suicide for their emperor.

The horror stories that we thought were made up just to scare us out of our wits when we first arrived came true as we fought our way from Australia to Japan through New Guinea, Biak, Peleliu Islands, Philippines, Okinawa and on towards Tokyo. This was the path to Tokyo that was the strategy of General MacArthur's command. New Guinea was a rugged island. It has a high mountain range running length wise down the middle of the island. Some mountains are 16,000 feet high. We could not fly over them in a C-47, because we had limited oxygen and that altitude was above the maximum ceiling of the aircraft. We had to find various mountain passes to fly through. When we flew through a pass we did not have much clearance over the ground. If we ever had engine trouble in the middle of New Guinea, they would never find us. There were no helicopters for rescue work during WWII.

When I looked down into the tropical rain forest I would wonder who lived in this jungle?

Looking down when we were close to the ground, we saw a number of wondrous sights. In the low country we saw different kinds of birds. Some were white parrots that were a contrast to the dark forest. There were more multi-colored birds of all types, maybe some were rare species; they were beautiful to watch flying over the jungle. When we went through a pass one time I saw a whole village of natives standing in an open space with their families and spears, looking up at us as if we were some heavenly higher order looking down on them. I will never know what they thought of our aircraft. New Guinea natives were one of the most primitive cultures that existed in the world at that time. I wanted to make a landing and find out myself what they thought of us, however I was always under orders to get our cargo from point A to B in the shortest time possible, and conserve precious fuel, so I never had an opportunity to do so. I was told later that most natives in that area were head hunters and I would probably never be found if I invaded their territory

WW II LOCATIONS OF THE "TOKYO TROLLEY"
375TH TROOP CARRIER GROUP WING
(55TH, 56TH, 57TH, 58TH SQUADRONS)

57TH TROOP CARRIER SQUADRON "BISCUIT BOMBERS"

375th, and 57th Morale Patches designed by Disney

DATE	LOCATION
18 Nov 1942	Activated, Bowman Field, Kentucky
2 Jun 1943	Final Training, Baer Field Indiana
31 Jul 1943	Port Moresby, New Guinea
2 Aug 1943	Dobodura New Guinea
20 Dec 1943	Returned to Port Moresby
22 Apr 1944	Nadzab, New Guinea
	BOB JOINED THE 57TH SQUADRON
23 Sep 1944	Biak, Schuten Islands
18 Feb 1945	Elmore Strip, San Jose, Mindoro
20 May 1945	Porac, Luzon
4 Aug 1945	Clark Field Luzon
20 Aug 1945	Kadena Field Okinawa
20 Sep 1945	Tachikawa, Japan
25 Mar 1946	57th TCS inactivated
Reference	See 57th "History"

CHAPTER 6

OVERLOADED TAKE-OFF

Bob: Under wartime conditions, you learned fast if you wanted to survive. Shortly after becoming a 1st Pilot I landed at a remote jungle airfield in New Guinea. I was bringing in a group of nurses, so they could take care of the wounded. After I landed, the air freight crew loaded me up with cargo to take to another outlying location. The cargo was heavy landing mat strips. The aircraft was a C-47 that had a maximum load capacity of 5,000 pounds. The air freight manifest said that I was loaded with 3,000 pounds of landing mat, however the mat was very heavy and didn't take up much space. The loading crew made a mistake and put on board a double load, 6,000 pounds, 1,000 pounds more than maximum. I was somewhere eating lunch and did not watch the loading.

When I came back to my airplane after eating lunch (10 in 1 rations, spam, coffee, and a wax chocolate bar, wax added so it would not melt in the jungle heat), I did not notice the extra heavy load. It was stacked on the floor of the airplane and was less than a couple of feet high. The Crew Chief who was supposed to be watching the loading, was sleeping and he didn't notice the extra weight. I stepped over the landing mat load on my way up to the cockpit. I asked to see the Air Freight manifest and it said that I had a load of 3,000 pounds.

There were always people who wanted to hitch a ride on my airplane to other bases in New Guinea. I thought I had only 3,000 pounds and told the operations officer over the radio to send out additional troops or nurses who wanted to hitch hike on my airplane. I accepted five additional passengers, estimated at about 1,500 pounds with their gear. I thought I had a load of 4,500 pounds, when actually I was loaded with 7,500 pounds of passengers and freight. The C-47 had a maximum take-off weight of about 35,000 pounds including a maximum cargo weight of 5,000 pounds. Without knowing, I was about to take off with 2,500 pounds over the maximum allowable weight.

As I taxied out to the runway, I sort of thought the airplane felt funny, not normal, but being a young hot pilot I didn't recognize that the problem was serious enough to stop, and I continued on my flight plan. After completing my preflight checkout, checking the magnetos at full power, I taxied to the runway and lined up the airplane for takeoff. I could see it was a relative short runway lined on each side with tall jungle trees and straight ahead at the end of the runway was another wall of tall trees.

I was first pilot and responsible for the safety of the passengers, crew and cargo. I was sitting in the left cockpit with the column controls in my left hand and the two throttles (two 1,800 HP engines) in my right hand. I lined up my gyro compass to the runway heading (145 degrees) and set my altimeter to the strip elevation (100 feet mean sea level). I looked over at my copilot and he gave me a thumbs up that it was okay to go because he had completed his pre-flight check list. I called the tower and requested permission to take off. The tower responded with "#156 you are cleared to take off." I said over the radio to the tower "Roger— #156 is on its way and you have a good day."

For a short field takeoff you hold the airplane with the brakes, the brakes are on the pedals, and you rev up the engines to full power (2400 RPM, cruise is 1800 RPM) and when everything is at maximum you let go with the brakes and accelerate down the runway. I pushed the throttles to full firewall forward, let go the brakes and headed down the runway.

As the plane lurched forward I had to make steady rudder control corrections to stay in the middle of the narrow rough runway, while at full throttle. It was a very short field. The runway was only 3,500 ft. long. Not long enough to have any comfort at getting off the ground even in a normal light load condition.

As I was heading down the runway, I was watching the trees in front of my airplane get closer and closer. I glanced at my airspeed: 50 mph, (at that time we did not use knots.). My tail was up off the runway. The C-47 had a tail wheel. It was configured as a three point landing type aircraft. At this point the aircraft felt a little heavy, not enough to let me know for sure that I had a problem. The C-47 can fly at about 85 or 90 mph.

About 3/4 of the way down the runway, my airspeed showed 85 mph and I was about to run out of runway. No problem, this was still looking like a normal takeoff. I gently pulled back on the column, to lift the nose of the aircraft and leave the runway. The aircraft did not respond. I recognized immediately at this point in the takeoff that something was wrong. The runway was being used up very quickly. The airspeed hit 90 mph and still no indication of flying. A quick glance at the copilot did not give me any additional confidence. He just shrugged his shoulders, but I knew that we were in trouble. The runway had run out. We were not taking off and there was no room to stop, we were going to crash into the jungle trees a few hundred feet ahead. The only thing that crossed my mind was, what can I do to make this airplane fly? I called to the copilot, or more likely screamed to him at the top of my voice, "give me 1/4 flaps and pull the gear up." He responded with "you have 1/4 flaps and the gear is up." There was a shudder, and the normal noise of the landing gear hydraulics and the flap actuators following the copilot's commands, but the airplane did not drop or gain altitude. We just stayed level with trees looming up in front of us. The airspeed indicator still read 90 mph and I could feel that the airplane finally was flying. It was very sluggish and felt like it was about to stall. As I eased the column back a little, the nose pitched up, almost imperceptibly just a little, and we gained a couple of feet in altitude. The trees were looming up in my face, we were still going to crash into the jungle.

I saw a slot, to the left, in the row of trees. I decided to make a very shallow left bank with my left wing down and my right wing up, thinking maybe I could squeeze through. When you bank you lose lift, but by this time I was trying to push the throttles forward with all my strength.

I probably bent the throttle levers. To avoid losing more altitude I was slowly banking, watching my airspeed, still at 90 mph. No reason to look at the altimeter or rate of climb instruments at this point in the takeoff, because they have too much lag time. My left wing was about 25 feet off the ground. We were actually in a flying turn when we passed through the slot in the trees. A few branches and lot of leaves were cut off by my left wing tip that was brushing the top of the trees. My right wing tip was clearing the trees on the right. We made it! Just beyond the trees was a 1/4 mile of tall jungle and then there was the coast line. Blue Pacific Ocean, no more obstacles, just open space.

The tower called me and said, "#156 what's your problem? Do you need assistance?" I radioed back and said "I'm SNAFU and will need to return. Please give me landing priority." (SNAFU was a military term that translated as "Situation Normal, All F—ed Up").

I still didn't know what my problem was. I could not continue on my approved flight plan to the next island over water without knowing what was wrong with the aircraft, and I was too overloaded with fuel to make a landing back on the short field, even without the extra weight of landing mat. I called the tower and operations and told them "I think I have an overload problem and I will fly around and burn off some fuel before I attempt to make a landing." I flew around the landing pattern so many times I was getting dizzy. Needless to say when I finally landed about 2 hours later I raised hell with my crew chief and with the air freight ground commander. I had the airplane unloaded. Later, with the same passengers, who seemed to accept the delay without much concern, I flew them and their cargo to the original destination. It was just another day in the life of a young C-47 troop carrier pilot.

As I mentioned earlier, I was 19 years old when I first soloed at Wickenburg's Primary Training base in Arizona. Nine months later I was commissioned as a second Lieutenant in the Army Air Force and was ordered to go to Instructors School at Randolph Field in Houston, Texas. By that time I had over 200 flying hours as a student, with over 600 landings. When I embarked to go overseas, I had 98 hours as a first pilot. After arriving in New Guinea in mid-October, 1944, we had our first ride, ever, in a C-47A type aircraft. During the last week of October 1944, I had four flights totaling five hours as copilot, and made five landings in this new plane. After that, it was off to war, so to speak. Things escalated rapidly, as can be seen from my flight logs for the next several months:

Month	Fly Days	1st pilot hrs	Copilot hrs	Landings
November '44	12	0	66	31
December '44	10	3	49	31
January '45	16	20	82	66

I suppose you could say we had a steep learning curve. It is not an exaggeration to say that you either learned fast, or died trying. In January we also started flying the C-46D Curtis Commando, a larger, faster aircraft. The C-46 could carry greater loads longer distances, but the C-47 continued to be used in remote areas with shorter landing strips. I had earned my 1st Pilot rating. Through February, March, and April, I flew about half and half 1st Pilot or copilot. By May, I was flying 100% of the time as 1st Pilot and later did flight instruction for new pilots as well. By the end of my time overseas I had accumulated over 1200 hours of flight time, of which over 90 hours was classified as combat flying. Before the war ended I was in the air on average every other day, sometimes twice a day, and made 460 landings on over 40 airfields in the South Pacific, most of them improvised jungle strips on islands in eight different countries.

From Boroke Airfield, Biak Island, I made a number of short hops to nearby islands such as Noemfoor and Owi, and also back along the east coast of New Guinea. Towards the end of the month I was making longer over-water flights to Morotai Island, Peleliu and Anguar Islands, then to Leyte. I logged combat time on the flights to Leyte.[4]

In November, the first 57th Squadron planes had flown to Leyte, landing at Tacloban Airfield in support of the campaign to take back the Philippines from the Japanese. Soon we had a lot of flights going to Leyte. We ferried supplies in support of our forward forces that had landed there on October 20th, 1944, about a week after I arrived in New Guinea to join the war.[5]

When flying into Tacloban, which was used as the front line landing area during the invasion, we were instructed by Tacloban's control tower to maintain our position in their landing pattern until all the fighters returning from their bombing missions got back down on the ground. Many of the fighter aircraft (P-47's) were shot up and low on fuel, As I circled in the landing pattern watching the P-47's land, I was amazed to watch the overall method of keeping the runway open. When a P-47 made a bad landing because it was damaged, to keep the runway open for the next fighter which was low on gas, the ground crew would just push the fighter aircraft off the runway into the adjacent sandy beach using skip loaders and bulldozers. After all the fighters were on the ground the Troop Carriers were then allowed to land. Just think about how surprised I was watching this runway cleaning method as I was awaiting my time to land, unload my cargo, and refuel for the flight back to Peleliu. What a waste of junked P-47's, however most of the pilots were saved to fly another mission by this method.

P-47 Fighter

CHAPTER 7

LIFE ON BIAK

During my six months on Biak, we lived in and flew around this beautiful tropical rain forest. It was beautiful to the eyes, but day to day living was very uncomfortable. It was too hot, too humid, too damp and just a terrible place to get comfortable on the ground. We all preferred to fly missions, because living in the airplane was more comfortable. We carried all our supplies with us. We had 10-in-1 food rations which contained various selections of canned goods. Meat, stews, vegetables and some goodies like puddings and gum and waxy chocolate bars. Cigarettes were plentiful. We carried folding cots and blankets to sleep under the airplane at night when we landed at a remote location. Some of the things we did were very innovative. When we were in need of cooling our bottled drinks, I don't think canned drinks were invented yet, we would do one of two things. We would tie a bottle on a string so that we could twirl it around over our heads. If we wrapped the bottle in an old rag and poured aviation fuel, 100 Octane gasoline, on the rag and then swung it around overhead the evaporating fuel would cause a cooling effect and we would have a cool drink. However, it probably took more energy than was worthwhile without giving an adequate return. The other method was to put our drinks in the airplane and take them up to a high altitude to cool them off and then make a fast descent back to the base before they warmed up again. We usually had a jeep meet incoming airplanes at the end of the runway to pick up cold supplies and deliver cool drinks to the squadron area.

Aviation fuel was available for many things. We used it to make hot water showers with a very dangerous gasoline burner contraption

Showers

using 50 gallon drums and pipes. It worked, but it had a potential explosive condition and I didn't like to be the one who fired it up.

When we were assigned a mission, we had to preflight our aircraft and make sure that the fuel did not contain too much water. The filler caps were up on top of the wing, and underneath the wing were little drain cocks that could be opened to drain the bottom of the tanks. Water has a specific gravity of 1.0 and 100 Octane gasoline is about 0.8 (floats on top of water). The water was supposed to collect on the bottom of the tank. When we opened the drain cocks we let the fuel spill onto the ground. The method was, let the fuel run over the palm of your hand and watch for little bubbles which indicated water in the gasoline. When the bubbles stopped forming we assumed that all the water had been eliminated. This was not a very foolproof method but it is still used in today's private piston aircraft. With jet engines it is not as critical, in fact a little water at the right time will add thrust to a jet engine, but conventional piston engines are much more sensitive to having water in their fuel. They just quit.

Because cigarettes were usually allocated freely, most of us smoked too much. We had Zippo type cigarette lighters. We used 100 Octane fuel as lighter fluid. When we drained the sumps after the bubbles stopped forming, we filled up our Zippo's.

Whenever we moved our base, one regular challenge was that of making a new camp. It was of some importance to put up shelters as quickly as possible to protect our few precious belongings from the unpredictable weather. Sometimes my airplane was the only option. For a more permanent, camp we used canvas tents when available. This meant clearing and leveling the land and pounding in stakes to support the tent against wind and rain. If local natives were standing around observing us, we could sometime pay them do some of the heavy work. Usually we followed Army protocol when setting up camp. This included digging heavy duty latrines as soon as possible. We learned by experience to place them down wind and as far away as practical. In the dense tropical forest, distant latrines meant a trek into a jungle known to be inhabited by Japanese stragglers, so we always carried a weapon. At night it was more complicated because the vines, bamboo and dense shrubbery made the path almost invisible and a flashlight was essential, even though it made us a potential target.

On Biak our first living quarters were pretty bad, just a shack. There was a mess hall where we got our meals, but they weren't much to brag about either. We had a jury-rigged outdoor cold shower. Bathroom facilities were latrines out in the jungle near the airfield. One night I visited the latrine, a loaded 45 in one hand and a flashlight in the other. As I took a seat, I turned off the light to save the batteries, set it beside me on the bench and sat gun in hand, listening for any strange sounds in the semi-quiet jungle. When I stood up, I heard rather than saw the flashlight roll and drop into the unpleasant depths of the single hole.

With no flashlight to use to look for it, I cussed at myself for having put it there and then cussed some more for having turned it off so I could not see where it landed.

But I had to have it. It was not as though I could stop at a hardware store and buy another. Flashlights were a scarce commodity in the jungle at that time and I was not about to lose mine! I found a piece of bamboo and probed around. Once I struck something hard I left the pole there and picked up another, thinking that maybe I could use them like chop sticks to pick up the flashlight. But the object I found was very slippery and constantly dropped out. I finally faced the music and hung head down as far as I could reach and eventually got hold of it. As slick and smelly as it was, fortunately it still worked and guided me back to camp where I cleaned it and myself at the first available water.

Life on Biak was not all work. When I was not flying a few of us would go around the local area to see the sights. We didn't want to go too far into the jungle because there were Japanese fanatics that did not want to surrender and were hiding out in caves and underground bunkers. We only had a suicide charge from them a couple of times and then they were quiet and we forgot all about them. But, being a young bunch of hot pilots we always tried to see what kind of trouble we could get ourselves into. There were a few back roads cut out of the jungle that were okay for a jeep or truck, but we did not always have a vehicle available to use in our leisure time.

We tore down our old shack and built a new house. It had a floor, a tent roof with a parachute inside for a ceiling, and all the walls were screened in. It was one of the best on the island. We would bring nurses over, cook dinner, and even had a record player so we could dance. One night we had a big party in our new house. We served scotch and water, and rum and Coke. Just about everybody in the squadron stopped by. I had a date with a cute nurse who was really nice. One problem was that the nurses were all at least 23 years old and a lot were older. When I went out with them, I felt like a little kid. Anyway, we had a good time. We also sent a ship to Sydney Australia to bring back stuff for the Squadron Christmas party. We hoped it would be a good one! Since I don't remember details, it must have been a great party.

One day a pilot who was going back to the States gave us a homemade boat. It was made from the bottom half of an old tear drop auxiliary fuel tank. The previous owner had scrounged up a gasoline powered washing machine motor and mounted it on the tank, and then made a propeller out of scrap aluminum. We worked on it to add a makeshift steering mechanism to control the rudder. Having a boat was of great interest, because with it maybe we could find our way up the coast to the nurses' quarters at the Army Hospital. The nurses' quarters were off limits from the road side entrance and the camp had high barbed wire fences all around. This boat construction kept us busy for a few weeks but we were dedicated to circumvent the off limits by approaching the nurses' quarters from the sea.

The Hospital on Biak

My friend and I dressed for swimming with our shorts on and loaded all the goodies we could scrounge into our "boat." We headed up the coast, putt-putting along in our new contraption with not a care in the world. We were headed about two miles up the coast to the Army Hospital area, because we wanted to find the nurses' camp and show off our boat or maybe give a ride or two to the nurses. They had a camp that was right on a sandy beach that was located in what we could call "a romantic tropical island paradise." Tall coconut trees, swaying in the breeze, white sandy beach and a clearing behind the trees with rows of tents for the nurses. As we neared the nurses' camp we caught sight of several nurses waving at us. They were wearing bathing suits. This was a rare sight for a couple of hot pilots. We beached our boat right in the middle of their sunbathing area. We were greeted with open arms and we were quickly outnumbered by about 10 to 1. They were all amazed and curious to see our boat and take a ride.

We were in paradise! We spent several hours lying on the beach and giving short rides in our wing tank boat and trading stories about back home in the states. It was getting late into the afternoon and we decided we had better head back to our camp at the

Bob and Friend find Paradise with Nurses

air strip. About half way back we ran into trouble. As we were chatting about how we were going to keep this special location to ourselves and come back every time we had a day off, we lost control of the boat. The steering mechanism broke and we were going around in circles in the ocean about a mile offshore. At this point along the shoreline there were steep 100 foot cliffs with no beaches, just rocks. We tried and tried to fix the steering and in the process the boat sank. It was all metal with no ballast at all. It went down fast. We were now all alone about a mile offshore and did not have any life preservers or debris from the boat so we started swimming towards the cliff. We were not great swimmers and we were very tired from trying to fix the boat. We never thought that it would sink and we would have to swim for our lives. For a while I didn't think I could make it. We both were struggling to stay afloat, gasping for air after our boat and all our possessions, our extra clothing, wallets and some left over goodies for the nurses had quickly disappeared from sight. We were now all alone miles away from any possible help.

It turned out I was a little better swimmer than my friend and I noticed that he was really having trouble breathing and staying afloat. I was extremely worried and thought that he would not be able to make it. My concern for him made me forget my own problems of being tired and out of breath. I didn't want him to drown and my concern for his safety gave me an extra shot of adrenaline. As we worked our way towards land I stayed close to him treading water and holding him up periodically, still worried that he would give up and sink out of sight. Every few yards as we paddled toward the shore I would ask him if he was all right. He always sounded and looked like he was not going to make it. He never said anything coherent, he just gurgled an "uhuh" with water caught in his words and a definite shortness of breath. Somehow I helped him make it the whole mile with just enough combined reserve energy to pull both of us up on the coral rocks at the base of the vertical cliff. I wasn't sure if we were going to survive and be able to continue on with our flying. I felt compelled to get out of this predicament so we could continue doing our small part in fighting the war against the Japanese.

We each were sprawled out, exhausted, almost naked, on top of large coral rocks at the base of a shoreline cliff, trying to recover our energy. It must have been the warm tropical sun and our youthful resilience that finally brought us around to talking about what we were going to do next. Here we were, a long way from help and without any survival equipment to get us back to our base. We visually searched the vertical 100 foot cliff in front of us and decided to try climbing up to the top and then work our way through the dense jungle, to a road that was about a quarter of a mile inland, and then by following the road we could find our way back. We were both now feeling better, but the exposure to the elements and our nakedness made us feel very vulnerable to all the dangers that lay ahead. We needed to figure out how to work our way back through the jungle to the road and then another 2 or 3 miles to our squadron area. We even thought about what our commanding officer would say about our next promotion after he found out about what happened and what stupid kids we were.

We spotted a potential route up the cliff, but it looked pretty dangerous. We were going to have to pull ourselves up the cliff hand over hand for most of the way. As we climbed up the cliff, our hands and feet were getting cut up by the sharp coral rocks. We didn't realize that our feet without shoes were vulnerable to such abuse. We had to work our way up slowly, grabbing foot and hand holds. There were a few plants growing out of the coral that we used as resting spots. As we got higher up on the cliff we tried to avoid looking down, however we had no choice but to continue up and up until we got to the top. We arrived at the top with bleeding feet and raw hands. We both learned that shoes are extremely necessary for survival. We also worried about coral infection. Cuts from coral usually ended up in a fungus infection that was difficult to cure in the rain forest climate.

After congratulating ourselves for the successful climb, we looked about at the dense jungle that we had to get through next. There were no visible paths and we could see that without much covering our bodies we would also be susceptible to all kinds of tropical bugs, animals, and diseases. Not a good feeling at all. Our feet were a major problem. After resting, our feet became even more sensitive, making it difficult to walk. We decided to use our American ingenuity and make ourselves makeshift shoes out of the nearby vegetation. We ripped up some banana leaves to obtain thin strips of fiber to use as string ties and then we wrapped the broad leaves around our feet and secured them with the string ties. Feeling pretty good about the fact we could make walking easier with our makeshift sandals, we headed into the jungle. We assumed that we could keep our direction straight and we started on our way inland where we could find a road home. The jungle underbrush was brutal, beating against our bare skin.

Our progress was slow and tedious. We were getting cut up by sharp plants and trembling from the spider webs that brushed against us as we pushed forward. We saw a number of colorful birds flying through the trees above us, but they didn't give us much peace as we had to brush off all kinds of crawling bugs that landed on our bare skin. It was a scary time. We visualized in our mind all kinds of snakes and jungle animals attacking us that we would have to fight off with our bare hands.

After about an hour of clawing our way through the jungle we stopped to figure out if we were lost. It felt like we had spent all day in the jungle, not just an hour. We were hungry, sore and cut up, and feeling pretty grungy. We looked like a couple of jungle natives who hadn't taken a bath in months. After debating what direction we should take by estimating from the sun rays and guessing the late afternoon time, we resumed our trek through the jungle until we finally emerged into a clearing and found the road that connected the airfield to the hospital. We staggered along the road, looking pretty tired and forlorn. After we had proceeded towards the landing strip, we heard a motor vehicle coming in the distance. We waited and waited, and as it approached we waved our arms frantically for it to stop. I wonder what the truck driver thought at first when he saw two grungy-looking natives with their hands in the air waving excitedly like they desperately needed help, but looking like they were too white to be from one of the local villages.

The truck driver stopped and looked down at us, not believing his eyes. We looked up and told him we were pilots in the troop carrier squadron and lost our clothes in an accident and that we had worked

Jungle Rescue

our way from the coastal cliffs through the jungle and we needed a ride back to the air base. After mumbling something about young flying officers always needing someone to help get them out of trouble, he asked us if he should take us back to the hospital so they could patch up our wounds. We declined saying we were all right and just wanted to get back to our squadron. He told us to hop in and he would get us back so we could go see our own squadron flight surgeon. He probably meant for us to have our heads examined.

As he let us off at our squadron headquarters we were viewed by our fellow officers and crew members as a couple of unrecognized jungle rats. We thanked the truck driver and offered him a ride around the island in a C-47, when we had a local training flight scheduled. He looked at us again and said, "No thanks. Bye-bye and have a good evening," as he drove off shaking his head.

I don't want to give the impression that we had a lot of free time and goofed off. During the month of December 1944 our flight operations concentrated on the Philippines. We flew to Leyte, bringing in supplies and bringing back the wounded. On December 20th, the 57th had its first flights to Mindoro—four days after the amphibious landings.[6]

Dispensary on Biak

We flew from Biak to Peleliu, unloaded, spent the night under the wing of the plane, re-loaded and re-fueled, and then went on to Tacloban Field on Leyte and back—8 hours of flying. They were still shooting on the ground so this qualified as combat flying time. On one of these long flights to the Philippines I began logging my first hours as 1st Pilot.[7]

As Christmas 1944 approached, we enjoyed two make-believe Christmas trees in the Chapel, made from jungle trees. They had strings of colored lights on them. We found some long socks, scrounged around to fill them with whatever we could find, and then hung them up Christmas Eve. The Mess Hall was decorated with strips of colored crepe paper. My friends Oscar, George, and Chet came over for a little get together with us. They liked our tent. I gave Chet some whiskey I had to trade for wood so he and his buddies could fix up their own tent. Oscar was across the road in a different group. It was the second time I'd been away from home for Christmas, the first time that I'd been overseas for the holidays.

I got a surprise when one of my best friends from high school and the Crystal Beach Gang, F. W. Clifford, came to visit. Clifford and I, when we were in the States, created a secret map. We took a map of the world and drew a grid system on top of it. On the vertical axis we wrote in a bunch of random numbers and did likewise for the horizontal axis. The numbers were not in numerical order. With this system, any square

Cliff visits Biak

on the map could be identified, and the numbers we used would mean nothing to anyone who did not have a copy of the map. For example, the square containing the Hawaiian Islands might have been identified as 19, 3. We would look on the horizontal axis for the column labeled 19, move down to the row labeled 3, and at the intersection find our location. Cliff and I each carried a copy of the map with us, so when we wrote to each other we could say exactly where we were. It was a pre-planned method of telling each other in letters where we were located without violating the normal censorship of our letters. He was in the merchant marine, and sailed on the SS *William C. Sublette*. When his ship came in on a supply run, he called around to try to locate me. He stayed over for

Christmas with me, and I took him on a tree-top training flight in a C-47 all around the island watching the New Guinea natives fishing along the shores next to their thatched huts that were located in the jungle close to the beach. Then we celebrated New Year's onboard his ship. We parted when his ship sailed back to the States. He promised to look me up again when the ship returned on its next Pacific assignment. Later, when I returned to the States and got married, Cliff was my best man.

Another year had gone by. Hopefully that meant that the war was that much closer to ending.

Lurking Danger: Only after photos were developed, did Bob and Cliff discover the native child they befriended held a hand-grenade.

CHAPTER 8

TROOP CARRIER MISSIONS

Troop carriers were the answer to a prayer for the fighting troops. We delivered supplies to the front lines when difficulties arose from the lack of adequate means of supplying our troops that were isolated by mountains and rugged terrain, far beyond reach of land or water transports. Troop Carrier planes, designed primarily for cargo purposes, could carry a great volume of freight to remote locations in a minimum amount of time. Our flying heavy loads of equipment and supplies from island to island played a significant role in winning the war against the Japanese aggressors. Our flying skills and activities not only reduced distances and time, but also reduced death rates and suffering of the wounded. The wounded must travel to base hospitals with optimum ease and speed. We made many risky flights, day and night, to accomplish our missions. Bad weather, enemy interception, and rough, jagged terrain were no deterrent to young dedicated pilots and crew using these sturdy, functional C-47 transports.

The Army Air Base on Biak was used as a major staging operation for moving troops forward in the fight towards the Japanese mainland. Biak was also used for training. We had additional flight training, paratroop drop training and glider towing training. We were always flying missions or training, so we were kept busy, without much free time. There was a paratroop unit camp not too far from our squadron. We worked with the paratroops on loading and jumping simulations, no actual jumps. All actual jumps were for real over enemy territory. Each of us took pride in accomplishing a dangerous mission. In fact we felt we were invincible and potential danger of a mission made it more of a challenge. The more dangerous the mission the prouder we felt in getting the job done.

Our feelings were captured in this poem written by my friend Russ Kibbe.

FORGOTTEN BUT NEEDED MEN

> You folks at home haven't heard of us.
>
> We aren't the boys who create all the fuss.
>
> We don't bomb and strafe and expect any glory,
>
> though rough flying to us is just an old story.
>
> We sweat out bad weather and enemy planes
>
> and with our cargo take many pains,
>
> especially with the much needed supplies
>
> and also the patients to save their lives.
>
> We fly hard hours on long-distance flights
>
> to come back to our base for tired restless nights.
>
> There are times on these flights we can return,
>
> but we have all come to learn,
>
> that the ship that we fly has to be our camp
>
> under the wing on a dusty ramp.
>
> So if you want the best man in the land,
>
> take the 57th squadron, Troop Carrier command.

Russ R. Kibbe, November 25, 1944, Biak Island

We got to know the paratroopers personally. We trained and played cards together, but when we actually dropped them in a forward area, we would not see them again until they returned months later regrouping for their next drop. The paratroopers were a tough group of guys that were willing to take a tremendous risk in jumping right into the middle of the enemy and fighting their way out. They always had a high casualty rate during each drop. We had a high regard for their bravery. They all talked like the next jump would probably be their last.

Many of our friendships were cut short from those who didn't make it.

A typical Operation in New Guinea involved the whole wing. When fighting for a new airfield we would fly over the Japanese-held territory, parachuting American paratroops and Australian artillerymen to seize the targeted Japanese airdrome and attempt to secure the perimeter of the airfield so we could land reinforcements. Once the runway was secure, we would land wave after wave of reinforcements. We would sometimes transport up to a whole division of Australian troops. When we landed and stopped on the runway, without turning off our engines, while under enemy fire, the troops would immediately jump out of the aircraft. As the Japanese bombarded us with mortar shells we would load the wounded and make a fast take-off, returning to our staging base for another return trip. The American and Australian ground troops would fight for the territory marching over the rough terrain, fighting through the jungle towards enemy encampments, overcoming any remaining Japanese resistance. We felt very lucky to be pilots, flying troops in and out, without getting involved in any direct combat. Being under fire was scary enough for us.

We had a particular problem one time when we were dropping para-troopers over the northern part of New Guinea. The drop altitude was determined by strategists evaluating the enemy forces, weather, winds and terrain. We were told to drop them at an altitude as low as possible. With the use of static lines, we could make successful drops at heights around 200-300 feet above ground. When a drop is made, the static line opens the chute and the altitude and wind conditions determine how the dangling paratrooper swings like a pendulum. Remember these were conventional parachutes of 70 years ago. The object was to hit the ground at the top of the swing where the landing impact would be minimized.

The aircraft with a full load had a stalling speed around 80 mph and we could fly at about 100 mph for these jumps. Also the paratroopers always asked us to drop them as low as possible, because they were easy targets from ground fire. The aircraft at 300 feet and 100 miles per hour made it easier to hit the target, but it was difficult and dangerous to fly so close to critical limits. If the airplane actually stalled out, there was not enough power to recover. In this particular mission the drop was miscalculated and we had an inordinate number of drop casualties, not from the enemy, but from our drop procedure. The combination of drop altitude, aircraft air speed, and wind condition all contributed to the worst possible condition, where the paratroopers hit the ground at the bottom of their swing. Unfortunately, they had the maximum impact on hitting the ground, causing too many casualties. Broken ankles and legs put many of the paratroopers into the hospital. Luckily the drop area was close to a landing beach and the marines were there at the same time and in a short time secured the area from the Japanese. The Navy quickly recovered the injured paratroopers and treated them back aboard their ship. Needless to say the paratroopers were not very friendly on their return to Biak.

Paratrooper Drop

Daily routine squadron flying missions were scheduled by the squadron Operations Officer. Our squadron mission information came from Wing headquarters and from the 5th Air Force Command Headquarters. Each element fighting in the Pacific followed orders from General MacArthur, our Supreme Commander who set the strategy for the Pacific war against the Japanese. Our Operations Officer was responsible for assigning pilots and crews to specific squadron aircraft. He also scheduled our cargo to some destination airfield nearby a fighting unit that desperately needed supplies, such as food and ammunition or replacement troops due to heavy losses.

Loading a Jeep in a C-47

The destination often was more than a single leg and it was the responsibility of the pilot to establish the flight plan and to chart a course with refueling stops. Needless to say when a hospital with nurses was not too far off course it always looked good as an overnight refueling stop. The return trips from the forward area brought back the critical wounded, personnel that were being reassigned, and those headed back to the United States because their tour of duty had been completed. The critically wounded were accompanied by nurses. During overnight stops we felt an obligation to entertain the nurses, so they would feel better about taking another long flight in our noisy aircraft. The stop over entertainment was usually a sightseeing trip around the base scrounging for anything good to eat or drink. The best source was usually found at the Navy Seabees (Construction Battalion) Quarters, or at the Army Base Hospital.

With the coming of the New Year (1945), we were busier than ever. We were starting to make the transition to the C-46 Commando aircraft. Then there were rumors that we were going to move the Squadron to Tacloban, but the move was cancelled. With the increased activity, we unfortunately experienced more accidents—six in this one month alone. In one, a taxiing B-24 bomber hit one of our planes that was attempting to land. The pilot was injured but there were no fatalities. On January 9th, 21 planes set out to move the 22nd bomber Group from Peleliu north to Samar Island. One plane, with four crew members, disappeared and was presumed lost. Several weeks later the wreckage was found in a swamp on Biak. The entire crew perished. The pilot was Thomas H. Fletcher. Sadly, he had been among the crews selected to be "First into the Philippines."[8]

Meanwhile, I flew over 100 hours that month, in the air four or five days each week. I increased my 1st Pilot's hours and also had my first flights in the C-46D aircraft. We did some glider tows, but almost all the flights were to either Samar or Leyte in the Philippines.[9]

Around the middle of February there was a very successful paratroop operation. Paratroopers were dropped on top of Corregidor, while amphibious troops stormed ashore on the lower levels. The 57th continued to supply the troops by air. Also, the 57th Squadron prepared to move from Biak to Mindoro, to better provide close in air support for the Philippines campaign.[10]

CHAPTER 9

GLIDER TOWING

Troop carriers were capable of very diversified missions. We could load the versatile C-47's with all kinds of cargo, such as large 2000 pound bombs (2 or 3 at the most) to fly to the forward bomber squadrons for bombing Japanese positions as we fought our way north. We could carry paratroopers for invasions from the sky. And we could transport medical personnel and Army nurses to and from remote fighting areas.

To increase our total fighting capability, we had WACO CG-4A gliders, each of which was capable of carrying up to 10 fully equipped airborne fighting troops. These were fragile craft made out of wood. We trained how to tow the gliders into a forward area, cut the gliders loose for a free fall landing on some open grassy area right in the middle of an offensive operation. Upon a successful glider landing the airborne infantry troops would jump out of the glider right into the middle of enemy territory requiring hand-to-hand fighting. We did not use the heavy wooden gliders in the subsequent thrust towards Japan. The gliders over time were abandoned and dry rot took its toll. Ground troops had to use bayonets and flame throwers to route the Japanese out of their concrete bunkers and underground caves. The Japanese did not surrender easily. We had to train ourselves to estimate all the variables so that when we cut the gliders loose they could glide (like a rock) into the target area.

We used paratroop drops and glider tows in the fight to capture New Guinea. Troop carrier pilots always thanked their lucky stars, that they could fly with relative safety back to their base, while they watched the gliders landing, one after the other, bracketing the target area like shotgun pellets, some gliders landed in the jungle but luckily most in the grassy areas. Most of the gliders were expendable and some of the airborne infantry we never saw again. As I have said before, we felt we were invincible and the potential danger of a mission made it more of a challenge. The more dangerous the mission the prouder we felt in doing the job, we were dedicated to win this war for everyone back home.

The Army Air Base on Biak was used as a major staging operation for glider operations. As a young pilot I was eager to learn how to take off a C-47 towing a fully loaded glider, a tricky operation at best. Starting with an empty glider I learned step by step. I started the operation by attaching a glider sitting on the runway to my aircraft using a single 500-foot-long nylon cord. The nylon stretched under load, making it behave like a bungee cord. These long bungee cords with one end attached to my C-47 tail would be laid out serpentine on the runway like a snake behind my aircraft with the other end attached to a glider about 100 feet behind. Both the glider pilot and I had independent disconnects to operate at our discretion.

My C-47, bungee cord and glider were positioned as close to the take-off end of the runway as possible to allow me the maximum takeoff runway length which was usually less than what the training manual required to get off the ground safely. Overseas we usually threw the book away and just did what we thought would work— usually taking added risks to get the job done. When everything was ready to go, I would radio the tower and say "X-ray 150 with glider is ready for takeoff." I would wait for the tower to respond with "X-ray 150 you are cleared for take-off." I had to rely on the tower assessment and the glider pilot to do the right thing. If at any time I felt that we were in trouble I could cut the glider loose, but there again was not much of a margin to avoid a dangerous aborted takeoff condition.

As I pushed the throttles full forward for maximum take-off power, I released my brakes. The aircraft surged down the runway, the glider still stationary awaiting the bungee cord slack to be used up. When the bungee became taught it stretched to about twice its original length before the glider started to move. When the glider started forward, the combination acted like a sling shot.

As the glider stretched the nylon tow line the glider would very

C-47 Towing Glider

quickly achieve flying speed and take off. The glider pilot would fly high above my aircraft. I was still on the runway trying to gain flying speed and I could not see what the glider was doing. The only way I could get enough

flying speed for a takeoff would be to have the glider pilot put the glider into a dive back down to the runway giving the tow line slack so my aircraft would have less drag from the glider. If this maneuver was done correctly I would be able to take off and fly at just above stalling speed. If the timing was off I would have to cut the glider loose and do my best to get the C-47 flying or stopped before the runway ran out. During training there were a lot of close calls, however after a while I learned how to do it with ease. The next step was to do the same take-off procedure with gliders fully loaded with troops and equipment. My first try was successful, but the C-47 would barely fly with a fully loaded glider.

I now had to practice cutting the glider loose in a position that allowed the glider pilot to land in the designated target area. This was practiced on a little island next to Biak. This island was not much bigger than a single runway. When we had our first fully equipped trial run we were not very good. We took off one

Troops in Glider Ready for Towing

aircraft at a time until we had about nine aircraft with gliders flying in formation of three groups of three each in right echelon. As we approached the targeted landing area flying downwind we would cut the gliders loose and the glider pilots would make a short 180 degree turn and land against the wind several hundred feet below. On this one trial the lead plane cut his glider loose, I was the second aircraft in this right echelon formation and several seconds later using seat of the pants judgment I cut loose my glider. This was followed by the third aircraft in the formation cutting loose his glider. The first glider landed in the target area, my glider pilot barely made the island, and the third glider landed on the sandy beach in a few feet of water. A couple of other gliders were dropped too far away and landed in deeper water. After we gathered up all our equipment on this little island we had to repeat the operation and make our return trip back to our base on Biak. This return exercise worked much better, all gliders were okay on the second try. We had no time for more practice. We were ordered to prepare for the real invasion of the next Japanese Island on General MacArthur's list.

We were personal friends with the glider pilots. We trained together, but when we actually dropped them in a forward area they became fighting infantryman. Just like the paratroopers we would not see them again until months later. The Airborne infantry and their glider pilots were willing to take a tremendous risk in landing gliders in the middle of enemy territory. They had a tough assignment, most were decorated for bravery.

Later, in June 1945 when we were stationed at Porac on Luzon, the 4th Glider Echelon was absorbed into the 57th Troop Carrier Squadron. Their training was carried out at Wakde Island. Captain George Allen, commanding officer of the glider group, played a lead role in one of the most amazing rescue efforts of the war. The story began in Hollandia. Fliers crossing over New Guinea had noted a remote valley populated by natives. It was given the name of "Hidden Valley" due to its remote and inaccessible location. As the presence of this remote area became known amongst the flyers and others it was named Shangri-La after the imaginary city described in James Hilton's novel "Lost Horizons." Due to the narrow canyon and high mountains surrounding the approaches to Shangri-La, it required extreme care to fly in for a look. On May 13, 1945 Colonel Peter J. Prossen flying a C-47A named "Gremlin's Special" took four crewmen, nine Women's Army Corps (WACs) personnel, and 10 male passengers on a sightseeing trip to see the valley. At a critical moment the pilot stepped out of the cockpit and left the flying to his copilot, who misjudged the height of the mountains rising in front of them. He tried to gain elevation, but the plane crashed in dense jungle on the mountainside. The pilot, copilot, crew, and most of the passengers died in the crash or shortly after when the plane caught fire. Two of the survivors died the next day, leaving three people, one officer, one enlisted man and one WAC as the sole survivors. Under the leadership of Lieut. John McCollom, himself a pilot, the three survivors made their way out of the mountains into a clearing, where they were spotted a few days later by search aircraft. Ironically McCollom's twin brother, Robert, was on the plane and died in the crash. All survivors were suffering from wounds and burns to greater or lesser extent. A C-47 dropped supplies and a radio so they could communicate their situation.[11]

A week later several rescue personnel parachuted into the site, including two medics. It became clear that extraction of the injured personnel and the paratroops could not be accomplished by land. A plan was developed to tow in a glider, position it for takeoff, and then "snatch it" with a C-47 that would fly in and grab its towrope with a long steel cable and a hook. The ground crew erected two tall poles on each side of an improvised runway. These poles held aloft a loop of the glider towrope. The C-47 aircraft had to descend to the proper altitude and snag the loop of the tow line while traveling at over 100 mph. As soon as the hookup was made the plane had to go to full power and climb to an elevation sufficient for it and the glider to clear the mountains at the end of the valley. The June 1945 Operations Report for the 57th Squadron provided this description of the daring rescue:

"Shangri-La is located 135 miles west southwest of Hollandia. The floor of the valley in the Orangi mountains, where it is believed that no white man had ever set foot previously, is about 5,000 feet above sea level. Its natural situation made the mission extremely precarious. Yet, it

was attempted since it was estimated would take months for an overland evacuation. Capt. Cecil Walters of the 11th Airborne Division and 10 Filipino paratroopers, including two medics, parachuted to the mountainside scene of the crash shortly after it happened some six weeks ago. An airline distance of 10 mile developed into 46 miles of travel overland before the party reached an area suitable for a glider to land and subsequently be picked up by a C-47 flying overhead. The Filipinos cleared an area of 100 x 400 yards, of which a strip 50' x 400' was firm enough to stand the weight of the glider without bogging down. It was necessary to make three trips into the Hidden Valley to bring out all the personnel, which included Lt. J. S. McCollom, T/Sgt. Kenneth Decker, and WAC Cpl. Margaret Hastings, survivors of the crash; eleven paratroopers, and an Australia war correspondent who, five days previous to the glider evacuation, and joined the rescue party via parachute.

"A total of six attempts were made but three were incomplete because of the weather. Outside of the landings and pickups in the valley, the greatest difficulties were encountered in the let-down over Shangri-La when the plane had to weave in and out of canyons and valleys to avoid clouds which shielded the mountains. One of the pickups was accomplished under extremely hazardous conditions caused by 500 foot ceiling. In order to use the snatch pickup system of takeoff, two strips of steel landing mat were placed under the wheels of the motorless plane. The glider pilots assembled the pick-up station and Capt. Ted Scholl, 8th Combat Squadron piloted his C 47 pickup plane throughout the operations. Because of obstructions, it was necessary to land the glider one direction, turn it around and set up the pick-up station for takeoff in the opposite direction." [12]

This rescue on June 28, 1945 received a lot of attention because of the Australian War Correspondent who took part. He parachuted into the site, reportedly never having jumped from a plane previously. It was said that he landed "half-smashed," having fortified himself with whiskey before making his first ever parachute jump. WAC Cpl. Margaret Hastings went back to the States to recover from her injuries. She never returned to New Guinea, but instead toured the U. S. to encourage people to buy war bonds.

CHAPTER 10

PELELIU ISLAND

Converting the standard twin-engine Douglas DC-3 to a troop carrier or cargo aircraft involved removing the comfortable passenger seats, all the interior soundproofing material, and any other unnecessary decorative materials that were only extra weight The seats were replaced with hard metal bucket seats that could be folded up out of the way of cargo or litters for wounded. A wind drift instrument (downward looking telescope to look at land objects or over water white caps to determine wind drift) was added, as was a navigator's desk, his instruments and a glassine dome for taking celestial bearings. The aircraft was then renamed the C-47 "Skytrain" for military uses

There were holes in the plastic windows so soldier passengers could poke their Tommy guns (Roaring 20's Thompson machine gun) in case of an enemy attack. They were designed more for passenger morale than to effectively defend the aircraft. Everything silver (polished aluminum) was painted dull olive drab in camouflaging blotches. Reinforced flooring was added to accommodate a jeep, a 75-mm pack howitzer, or anything else of similar and feasible size and weight, such as the 2 1/2 - ton airborne truck.

The range of the C-47 Skytrain was 600-700 miles, depending on the total cargo weight. Most of our trips were over 500 miles point to point and often all over water or unfriendly territory. This meant that when the flight passed its midway point there was not enough fuel to return and if the weather was closing in at your destination there were no alternate airports. This point of no-return always made me feel anxious and I would listen to the radio reports sometimes telling me that my destination airport was closing. I had numerous close calls, a couple of which will be described in later chapters.

Another sensitive consideration was the aircraft performance. Several hundred miles over water, if I had an engine failure and had to ditch the plane no one would ever find the aircraft or its remains. The Operations briefing always had a number of aircraft and crew names that were missing along my route and I was asked to keep looking. I only spotted one, and that one crashed in the jungle, several days earlier. That particular flight was scheduled to fly equipment from Biak north about 700 miles across the equator to Peleliu Island. It was determined that the water truck being transported, was fully loaded with water and its overweight condition caused the plane to crash shortly after takeoff without anyone from the ground seeing the accident. All the passengers and crew were killed. I never heard of any plane lost over water in this area being spotted by subsequent over-flights or having its crew rescued at sea.

The Caroline Islands are part of a larger island group called "Micronesia" (small islands). They are located just north of the equator, between the Marshall Islands and the Philippines. The western-most group of islands is called Palau and Peleliu, a little island within the Palau group, was the western Pacific headquarters of the Japanese ground forces and was well fortified. U.S. invasion forces with U.S. Navy support had a bloody battle in capturing part of Peleliu and adjacent islands to establish airstrips for our offensive in invading the Philippines 600 miles over water to the west. The Japanese never did surrender. The U.S. just took possession of the airfields and surrounding area while the stubborn suicidal Japanese troops retreated into the hills and caves.[13]

As the U.S. forces moved north in MacArthur's "Island-Hopping" campaign, the Japanese troops on Peleliu and many of the other South Pacific islands were bypassed. Thousands were left stranded in their garrisons and caves. Since the American Navy had the area blockaded, the Japanese Navy could no longer bring them supplies or transport them to the front. They were left to "wither on the vine," to survive as best they could, to try to stay alive with little food and medicine, no longer a fighting force. After the war's end they would eventually be repatriated to Japan. Even then, there were those refused to believe the war was over, and stayed on as stragglers in the jungle. One soldier, Hiroo Obata, remained in the jungles of the Philippine island of Lubang until 1975, before finally surrendering.[14]

Every once in a while the Japanese would make a sneak suicidal attack. They would come from their caves in the northern part of Peleliu, to our airstrip in the southern part, coming down along the coast at night in makeshift boats. They would charge ashore with bayonets, trying to kill any of our troops they could until they themselves were killed. There was excitement on the morning of January 18th, 1945. It turned out that three barge loads of Japanese Marines attempted to land near our base on Peleliu. One barge pulled ashore several hundred yards from where my aircraft was parked on the airstrip parking ramp. I recall sleeping under the wing of my parked C-47. I was awakened by our vehicles and a nearby U. S. Marine infantry unit going by fully armed and firing their weapons towards the shoreline not too far away from the parked aircraft. I was startled and told to grab my sidearm and prepare for hand to hand fighting. After assessing the situation, I decided that the best plan was to get out of the way of our fighting troops so I ordered my crew to run the opposite direction towards the Headquarters buildings across the runway beyond the taxi strip. We did not know the strength of the Japanese landing force at the time. The Marines took care of most of them but a few managed to get to the interior of the island. They were subsequently hunted down by patrols. No matter how many there were, it was enough to scare the hell out of me. A constant guard was kept on the planes and they were not damaged.[15]

Our aircraft was not touched, so early the next morning we loaded the plane in the dark, refueled and took off at sunrise to return to Biak. I was happy to get in the air and away from Peleliu, however I subsequently made many trips back and forth over the equator taking supplies to Peleliu and bringing wounded back to Biak. I was involved in a few more suicide attacks, but fortunately never was injured.

Besides flying south from my home base in Biak into various airstrips in the New Guinea jungle and to surrounding islands along the New Guinea coastline, I sometimes flew west to the Halmahera group of islands (now part of Indonesia). However, flying north 600 to 700 miles across the equator to the front line forces on Peleliu and an adjacent little island called Anguar was most critical.

Traveling long distances over water, flying on instruments in bad weather, while expecting to find a little island just big enough to have an airstrip, was often a difficult navigation problem. We had a small crew consisting of the pilot, copilot, and usually just one other, who might be an engineer, radioman or navigator, depending on who was available. Our navigational aides were limited. We had pre-flight briefings on weather and airfield conditions, but most of the in-flight information was not very accurate. We had detailed maps, barometric readings, and information on potential thunderstorms that might be in our flight path. In addition we had a magnetic compass, airspeed instrument and outside temperature indicator. If conditions allowed us to see white caps on the ocean below, we could estimate our ground speed and wind drift angle.

Pilots used Maps, Instruments, Sight & Landfall Navigation

When flying on instruments with zero visibility we had to rely on our magnetic compass, clock, and airspeed information to do the best we could to estimate our time of arrival. Airspeed, with estimated wind speed and direction, allowed us to calculate ground speed and true direction and make a rough calculation of time of arrival. (Maybe!) The maximum range of the aircraft did not allow much room to correct navigational errors. So we would fly what is called a "land fall." Imagine if you flew directly toward an island with all of your best calculations and now you should be there, but the island was nowhere in sight. What do you do next when you only have enough fuel to fly another 100 miles? Do you continue to fly straight ahead, hoping, or change course? Left or right?

The "land-fall" method helped solve this navigational problem. It was not fool proof, but it gave the pilot a way to make an intelligent guess in this tense situation. It worked this way: All during the flight, with all calculations, using best estimates, you put an extra right or left (choose one) offset into your heading to try to insure that you miss the island on a predicted side. As an example: After flying for four hours over the ocean towards, say Peleliu island, when your calculations indicate that you should see the island and you only see ocean, you could be in big trouble. With the "land fall" method you should now know which way to turn to have the best chance of locating Peleliu.

We had a radio compass that could track radio broadcasts and give the direction of the transmitting station. The use of the radio compass was our best way to find a radio equipped island. However, if there were thunder storms, and being on the equator we always had thunder storms, the radio compass would leap to the direction of the lightning strike, swinging the direction needle in a random motion. We had to look at the needle swings and try to decide which direction was for the radio transmitter on the island

Hence, one of the most difficult jobs for the pilot was making sure that he arrived at his destination without running out of fuel and being forced to ditch the aircraft in the ocean, and endure all of the problems that would bring.

On one of my trips, flying 22 Army nurses from Biak to Peleliu, I was flying through very bad weather. The C-47 was bouncing around, like a cork on water, because of all the thunder storm activity. The nurses were complaining about getting airsick and were probably getting frightened. The C-47 could not fly any higher than about 12-15 thousand feet and as the thunderstorms extended to 30 thousand feet, I could not fly over them. Most of the four hours of flight time was without visibility and on instruments.

When we reached our estimated time of arrival, there was a small break in the clouds, but there was no island in sight. The nurses were anxious for me to land and get them on solid ground again. The crew and I were worried that we were not going to find the island at all. But we gave no indication to the passengers that we thought we might be in trouble. Because I had calculated a "land fall" for left, I had no choice but to turn left and continue on my way looking for Peleliu. There were periodic breaks in visibility in between the thunderstorms. Looking down anxiously through these breaks in the weather, the crew and I could not spot Peleliu, or any land at all.

I continued flying, planning how I might ditch the aircraft in the water and wondering when I should send out an S-O-S. I only had about another 1/2 hour of flight time. We had a radio compass that could track radio broadcasts and give the direction of the transmitting station. These contingencies were being discussed in the cockpit, while we were smiling at the nurses, trying to calm their nerves about the rough air, hoping they did not suspect that the problem was much worse. Suddenly, through one of the breaks in the clouds, I spotted an island, which was nowhere near my estimated location. But it sure did look good! I talked it over with the crew and we decided to turn toward that little speck on the horizon, where, in the worst case, or maybe only next to worst case, I could ditch the aircraft in shallow water and at least save the crew and passengers.

As we approached the island, we could see it only once in a while when the clouds opened up. Fortunately we were able to recognize it from our charts. It was one of the islands in the Palau Group. This gave me clear knowledge as to the direction to Peleliu. The fuel was getting dangerously low, but knowing that I could now reach Peleliu with about 10 minutes of remaining fuel, I turned for our target island.

As soon as I was able to radio the tower, I informed them that I was about to run out of fuel, so they gave me priority to land and I landed happily on Peleliu without any fanfare. The trip had been suspense-filled and tense for the crew and the passengers. I was emotionally drained. The nurses were glad to be on land again, but were never apprised of the potential danger of ditching in the ocean. After a debriefing session with Operations, and my discussion with other pilots flying the same route, it was determined that there was a tremendous tail wind that I was not able to estimate. Unknowingly, I had flown beyond Peleliu without seeing it and, after finding the other island, circled back to my destination. Thanks for the "Land Fall" method I turned in the right direction. Unfortunately this type of Island hopping soon became pretty standard procedure, with numerous other close calls.

All is well that ends well. We visited the Seabees with some of the nurses and had some good chow before we boarded our plane for the return to Biak.

Peleliu was the first place where I could say that I had intimate contact with the horrors of war. As mentioned above, we were acutely aware of the Japanese stragglers hiding in caves to the north of the airfield. They were defeated, but continued fighting. All around us were reminders of the conflict that had taken place there—the destroyed military equipment, shattered trees, empty supply boxes. When not flying we went off and looked in some of the caves for souvenirs; in hindsight, probably not a smart thing to do. We found a lot of Japanese Yen and sent it home in our letters because we were using occupation currency. When we reached Japan we were surprised to learn that those Yen were acceptable currency.

While the Japanese stragglers remained a danger during 1945, after the end of the war they retreated into remote hiding places and just struggled to stay alive. Many were repatriated to Japan in the early years following the war. Some remained in hiding for a decade or more. A Korean conscript named Keiki Tokugawa was finally captured on Peleliu and returned to Japan in 1955. In 1956, nine more stragglers surrendered on the island of Morotai. [16]

At the south end of the island there was a beautiful cove with crystal clear water. I went there several times for a swim to cool off and look for interesting shells to send home to my mother. One day while swimming I noticed a half a dozen yellow bricks of high explosive in the shallow water and decided it was time to swim elsewhere.

Recalling my own experiences on Peleliu, and researching some of the background for this book, brought back memories. I had a hard time sleeping thinking about the cruelty of that campaign.

Japanese Cave Hideout

PART III

MACARTHUR LANDS ON LEYTE • MOVE TO MINDORO: PHILIPPINE ISLANDS •MANILA TAKEN & POWS RESCUED •PREPARING MOVE TO OKINAWA • STAGING AREA FOR THE INVASION OF JAPAN.

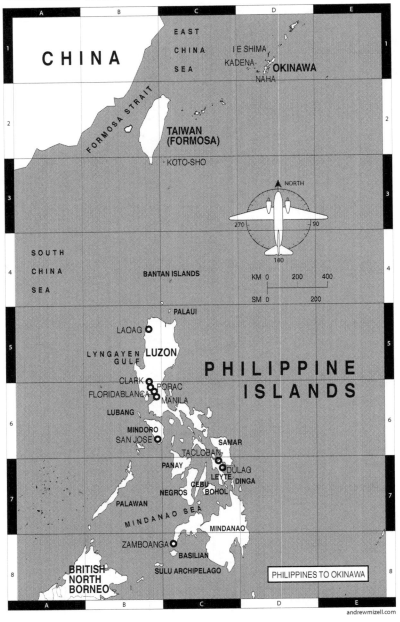

andrewmizell.com

CHAPTER 11

MOVE TO THE PHILIPPINES:
TACLOBAN, LEYTE AND SAN JOSE, MINDORO

We were carrying all kinds of supplies back and forth to Peleliu to get ready for the next leap to the Philippines. We were taking nurses into Peleliu and bringing back wounded from the fighting there. As MacArthur was making his famous landing on Leyte Island, several airfields were captured early-on to provide air cover for the invading U.S. Naval fleet and Army ground forces. These were the fields at Tacloban and Dulag. We began flying into Tacloban to provide support for the ground troops. When the fighting was intense, the airport was busy with fighters coming in and out. The transport planes had to circle at 3,000 to 5,000 feet until all the fighters were on the ground and parked off the runway. The fighters were usually low on fuel coming back from combat. Some crashed on landing

Tacloban, Leyte Island Landing

because they were shot up. At the airfield they had bulldozers and in an emergency just pushed the crashed planes into the ocean to clear the field so the next group of planes could land.

Dulag was another field south of Tacloban where I would fly in to pick up the wounded and take them back to Peleliu. One time I took off, looked at my right wing, and noticed my aviation fuel was blowing off, spraying like a fire hose from the top of the wing. It was gushing out of the wing tank—the maintenance guys had left the gas cap off the fuel tank and high octane aviation gas was blowing out. There was risk of fire or explosion at any instant, and with a heavy load of the wounded on board I was extremely concerned. I wanted to get back on the ground ASAP. I circled, re-entered the traffic pattern, and went back to make a short field landing with full flaps. There was a high hill—about 2,000 feet—at the end of the runway, so landing was always tricky there, but I managed to land safely. On board passengers were as happy as I was to be safely back on the ground. We did not have an intercom to notify the passengers of flight events, however we passed information to the Crew Chief on board and he would walk back to inform the passengers.

We spent the night under the aircraft wing, sleeping on a cot. Sometimes we could stay with local shore-based Seabees—they had the best food. At Tacloban, the Japanese had destroyed the city, and fighting was still going and there was lots of naval activity. Leyte Island was not declared secure until the last Japanese were defeated in January 1945, although mopping up of stragglers continued until July, 1945.

After the Leyte landings, Tacloban was a staging area for the capture of Mindoro, an island located south of Corregidor. It was the next stepping stone for the eventual recapture of Luzon. MacArthur knew that the island was poorly defended and could be used to provide air cover and transport for the forces that would be fighting on Luzon. We began flying supplies in and out of Tacloban, and landed there as a waypoint when the 375th Troop Carrier Group (squadrons 55, 56, 57, 58) were on their move to San Jose, Mindoro.

There was a major battle to take the airport at San Jose, Mindoro with paratroops. The troop carriers picked them up from staging areas and then dropped them down onto the enemy area. The pilots didn't know exactly the tactical details of the drop, just the time and place. Once the drop zones were seized, the island was quickly cleared by ground forces of enemy Japanese. The San Jose airport became an important base as a staging area for the subsequent invasion of Luzon. It played a critical role in providing air cover to ground troops and a base for supply.

The Japanese recognized the importance of the airfield. After the Americans captured the airfield, a group of several hundred Japanese soldiers was landed on Mindoro in December, 1944, with instructions to sabotage the air field. Their surprise attack failed and all but 30 were killed. The survivors fled inland, where their numbers dwindled to fifteen. They divided into two groups to be less conspicuous, but one group was attacked by natives and wiped out except for one man. The others constructed a farm on a remote mountain top where they managed to grow crops and remain largely unnoticed until 1956, when four remaining survivors were repatriated to Japan. [17] Such was the dedication and tenacity of our enemy. There was good reason for us to exercise care if we went very far from any of our jungle bases!

Once the San Jose airfield had been secured, we moved the entire squadron there. This was a very hard strip for take offs and landings. It was a dirt field and lots of times the dust was so strong that you couldn't see the end of the runway. Water buffaloes running across the field were another hazard. In a way we didn't mind the hardships. We understood that in each of these jumps forward, we were bringing the troops closer and closer to the Japanese home islands.

Water Buffalo, called Carabao

We flew many flights to supply the troops converging on Manila. These brought gasoline for vehicles, food and water, ammunition, and other needed supplies, while also evacuating the wounded, and later, freed POWs.

University of Santo Tomas Internment Prison.

Santo Tomas Liberation

C-46 Evacuating the Nurses out of Santo Tomas

CHAPTER 12

AIR RESCUE AT SANTO TOMAS

General MacArthur was concerned about American prisoners of war held by the Japanese in the Philippines. At that time the 57th was stationed on the Island of Mindoro, located south of Manila, in support of General MacArthur's forces as they fought their way, island by island, to recapture the Philippines as the next step towards defeating Japan. As the American troops advanced rapidly towards Manila, MacArthur gave orders that efforts be made to rescue American military and civilian POWs. This effort was complicated by the fact that the POW camps were located behind the front lines and were still under Japanese control. In spite of the dangers and hazards, four daring rescues were carried out.

On January 30th 1945, at Cabanatuan City north of Manila, United States Army Rangers, scouts, and Filipino guerrillas liberated more than 500 Allied and civilian prisoners. Later known as The Great Raid, this rescue effort liberated the prisoners while they were guarded by over 200 Japanese soldiers in an area surrounded by Japanese troops.[18] Next, a "flying column" from the U.S. Army First Calvary division sped towards Manila, bypassing blown out bridges, reaching España Street that fronted the Santo Tomas camp just about dusk. There, on February 3rd, a tank named *Battlin' Basic* smashed through the front door of the compound and the American GIs encountered 3,700 happy prisoners of war.[19] The next day more rescues took place in Manila when the notorious Bilibid Prison was liberated. Then, on February 23, another amazing rescue took place at the Los Banos camp, where American forces again came in behind Japanese lines to rescue more than 3,000 civilian POWs.[20]

Santo Tomas was located behind enemy lines in the city of Manila when the American forces liberated it. Initially the prisoners remained in the camp where the Army could feed and protect them as the battle for Manila raged on. On the 23rd of February, Gladys Savary, an American woman who had aided the POWs by smuggling food into the camp, visited Santo Tomas. She wrote: "That day in Santo Tomas was heart-breaking. They were so pitifully thin…" [21] In March, she noted, "The repatriation of the Santo Tomas and Los Baños internees has gone along quickly. The sick and the nurses were flown home first, and after that, ships, as they became available, took the rest." [22]

As it turned out I played a role in the Santo Tomas University rescue effort. Initially the POWs stayed in the camp where the Army could protect them, because there was still fighting going on nearby in the city. Some days after the camp was liberated we took-off in our C-46 aircraft from our dirt airstrip at San Jose, on Mindoro Island, where we were stationed. Our orders were to follow an earlier Troop Carrier mission that dropped the paratroops that helped capture a so-called rescue landing strip close to the Santo Tomas University. It turned out to be Quezon Avenue, a narrow, two-lane divided highway close to the University. Army engineers patched the roadway and tore down telephone poles where necessary. We landed with one gear on one lane, the other on the opposite lane, and the tail gear in the grassy median strip between the two lanes.[23] We were assigned to bring back to Mindoro as many women and children that we could safely load onto our aircraft. I recall as I was flying low over Manila, to avoid enemy detection, I looked down into the ancient walled city of Manila watching the Army ground troops fighting the Japanese, forcing them out into the open with flame throwers. I remember thinking I was so lucky to be flying and not on the ground in hand-to-hand combat. After watching the fighting action on the ground I became preoccupied in locating the highway that was our makeshift rescue landing strip. It was a narrow street, short and curved, a major highway in the city of Manila. In February we were flying C-46s almost exclusively. I was dividing my time equally between Pilot and copilot duties. [24]

As I recall, we flew in and landed near a place called Quezon Park and used the highway near Santo Tomas as our landing strip. I think there was a group of three planes. My landing on the highway was tricky but uneventful, however I was wondering how I was going to take off with a heavy load of women and children. As I taxied to

Highway used as a Landing-Strip
View toward the University & Manila

a parking area there was a number of Japanese snipers still fighting close by and shooting at us. The bullets missed my aircraft but they did wound some of the other aircraft crew members.

One of our pilots took off with 80 POWs, while I took off with 60 POWs. The difference in numbers was probably due to total weight and balance conditions of my aircraft. There was still fighting going on while we were on the ground. One of the pilots from the 55th squadron wandered too far away from his plane and was killed by Japanese snipers. This was combat flight time for sure![25]

For many of the passengers, this was the first time they had been in an airplane. Some of the children had never seen an airplane before. They were all thin and had evidently lost much weight during their long period of captivity. The Japanese really treated them roughly. They really didn't have words to tell us how happy they were. Later we learned that near the end they had been literally starving.[26]

It was heartwarming to see the interned families all waving and wanting to be first to get onto my aircraft. We loaded, no overloaded, the number of women and children that we could handle safely for a short field takeoff. We took off with jamb-packed passengers and safely flew them back to Mindoro. The passengers were so happy to be rescued. We were then briefed for our next mission and I never had much time to personally meet and talk to any of our rescued passengers. Many of our planes aided in the evacuation of Allied civilian and Army personnel who were interned after the fall of Bataan, Corregidor, and other bases in the Philippines.[27]

The link below shows the air rescue at Santo Tomas:

https://archive.org/details/InterviewingPhilippineInternees1945

Typical Thatched Home Philippines

C-47s Flying over Manila

C-47s in Philippines

CHAPTER 13

R AND R IN AUSTRALIA

W hen I landed on these forward bases such as the airfield in Peleliu Island, I had to endure sporadic night raids on the airfield. My crew and I would be sleeping under our airplane on cots and we would have to continually be on guard. We never knew when a group of fanatic Japanese soldiers would sneak out of their hiding place, usually hidden caves in the hills, or from another northern island in the same Palau group via makeshift boats, and come charging to attack the airfields. I was fortunate not to be involved with more than two or three of these raids during the time I was on the ground. Flight time in and out of the Peleliu Island group was considered forward combat zone flight time. As I flew back and forth over the equator between Biak and Peleliu Island I was logging combat time. Later, the same was true of the Philippines.

The Army awarded special medals to those having a certain amount of forward area combat zone flight time. Specifically the medals, in order of importance were: first the simple Campaign Medal, then with more combat hours the Air Medal, and then finally the Flying Cross. Along with the medals, each combat pilot was given leave for rest and recuperation (R&R).

After logging forward area combat time, I became eligible for an Air Medal. The medal would be presented at a formal ceremony, however the R&R awarded with the medal was usable as soon as you could find a replacement pilot. R&R was more important than a medal to a young

20 year old pilot. After living in a jungle environment for a few months most of us were looking forward to R&R that would allow a relaxing visit in a modern city with good restaurants and entertainment. That modern city was Sydney Australia located about 1000 miles south of Port Moresby, New Guinea.

I became eligible to go on leave in February, 1945, but then all leaves were abruptly cancelled. It made me mad that everybody else had been in Sydney—Kibbe, Parma, Headly—my tent mates. They all went while I had to stay behind and fly. Later, I supposed that the cancellation was occasioned by the Philippine campaign heating up and the move of our squadron from Biak up to San Jose, Mindoro. In any case, I was very surprised when I suddenly got my orders. I had just come back from a mission and the CO (commanding officer) told me to be ready to go on leave the next morning at 0530. As I recall, this was mid-March. My flight logs show no flights for the last half of March. I guess they didn't count flying on leave as "real" flight time.

I found another pilot who would fill in for me for the next week if when I returned I would do the same for him. I arranged to get assigned to a flight from Biak south to Port Moresby, New Guinea for the next day. The name of the airplane was "X157, Kings Cross shuttle." This same airplane would allow me to fly on south to Sydney Australia, only if I had an approved cargo to take to Sydney. I worked out a scheme with the Operations Officer to have a number of combat leave eligible non-flying officers and enlisted men that were anxious to take leave in Sydney. This trip was approved by the commanding officer, because the wounded needed to be evacuated for special treatment, even though a paradrop in the forward Halmahera area was his highest priority during this time.

Without any delay I loaded my airplane the next day with this group of rowdy soldiers ready to go raise hell in Sydney and with a cargo of wounded soldiers, their very attractive attending nurses, and a special cargo of spare parts to deliver to Port Moresby. When we were taking care of the wounded with their nurse support we would make sure that we had a place to party with the nurses when we stayed overnight at some remote base. Sometimes we would party overnight in the aircraft or go on a local tour to a nearby sandy beach. It was not difficult to find other U.S. Military organizations around the airfield that would host the party, like the Navy Seabees. U.S. nurses were a special treat to all the war-weary soldiers and sailors, especially to young hot pilots. My waypoints south, included the little island of Wakde (300 miles south), for refueling

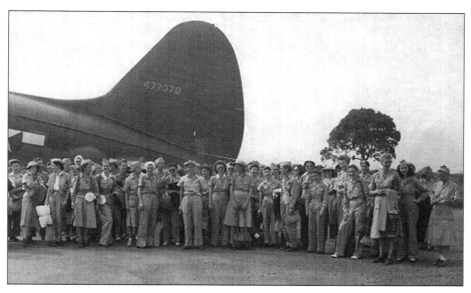

Nurses by C-46

and then on another 500 miles south to Nadzab, New Guinea to deliver spare parts. In the evening there we would have another party which always included several of the flight nurses. From Nadzab it was across the southern New Guinea peninsula to Port Moresby, where the wounded would be put on board hospital ships to return to the U.S. Unfortunately, at this point our lovely nurses would be reassigned to another mission.

C-47s Port Moresby

The trip south to Nadzab was uneventful but beautiful. From the air the New Guinea jungle was a plush green color of dense vegetation and

Wau Airstrip

it was easy to spot multicolored birds flying over the tropical canopy. The only worry on these flights was what would happen if we had a mechanical failure and had to make a forced landing in the jungle. We knew there was not much of a chance of surviving a crash in that jungle. Once your plane penetrated the treetop canopy, it became virtually impossible to see from the air. You would never be found.

When I landed at Nadzab, a short landing mat strip in the middle of the jungle, my flight plan was changed. We made arrangements to put the passengers, nurses and wounded up in the Base visitors quarters so that the aircraft could be diverted to another very seldom used airstrip in the middle of the jungle located on a mountain side with its runway hewed out of the dense jungle. I spent the night telling the nurses and Nadzab personnel stories about the operations up north and how we captured the Peleliu Islands, as if I did it, along with the nurses, single handed.

The next morning the flight crew and I took off for a one day trip to deliver spare parts to Wau air strip high up in the middle of the New

Guinea. Wau was under siege by the Japanese. Wau's life line was troop carrier C-47 "Sky trains" that unloaded troops, ammunition and supplies, while under heavy enemy fire, then returned with the wounded. My flight of spare parts was a light load specifically to allow for a safe landing on this unusual airstrip. The strip was on a hillside, its upper end was about 300 feet higher than the lower end and it was only 3,300 feet long. The landing had to be made uphill and the takeoff downhill. When I landed I thought that I was pulling up way too high and was worried about stalling out, but I somehow greased it in—just luck, I'd say. The landing roll was very short because of the 10% uphill grade. Needless to say, the local troops that were defending Wau were always overjoyed to get needed supplies. The spare parts were quickly unloaded and replaced with wounded personnel. In less than one hour I was ready to return to Nadzab for another evening with the nurses.

There was little enemy fire and I was ready for my first critical downhill take-off. This was a very unusual attitude for the aircraft and especially a new experience for me. This 10% slope doesn't sound like much but looking out of the cockpit with the tail on the ground the far end of the runway looked like it faded away into nothing. There was also a strong cross-wind which would make the take-off even more troublesome. After making sure that the wounded were strapped in comfortably, I called the makeshift tower, a radio operator in a jeep, and requested take-off clearance. He answered, "X-ray 157 you are cleared to take-off."

I responded with "Roger, 157 returning to Nadzab, have a good day—take care." I then headed down the runway with full throttle, as soon as I lifted the tail off the ground my attitude felt normal, however the acceleration of the plane was unusually fast and the crosswind forced the aircraft to veer off course. With strong rudder control and no flaps the airplane overcame the crosswind and started to fly; in a very short roll I had flying airspeed. I had to avoid my normal take off instrument readings because I was losing altitude and instead of climbing out I was diving out. I relied on my airspeed indicator and when my airspeed was adequate I climbed out, circled the field, and headed back to Nadzab.

This kind of takeoff must be something like taking off from an aircraft carrier. On a carrier the catapult gets the aircraft almost up to flying speed, but the aircraft drops off the end of the carrier deck and loses altitude before recovering its normal flying attitude. I felt like I had been qualified for a carrier take-off.

Back in Nadzab we rejoined the original group, which included several nurses, for an evening of poker. Early the next morning we took-off again for Port Moresby, and hopefully, this time, to go all the way to Sydney Australia.

Port Moresby and Dobodura were two landing areas south of Nadzab, in the southern-most portion of New Guinea. Dobodura was located on the Eastern seacoast and Port Moresby was located on the Western coast. Port Moresby therefore was the natural stop over spot for an over water flight south to the Australian Continent and on to the city of Sydney.

Typical Thatched Home

The stopover in Port Moresby was always interesting because of the natives. The Papuans were descendants of the aboriginal inhabitants and had retained their language and customs. It was always a question in my mind as to whether the natives entertained us or we entertained them with our Yankee customs. The Papuan natives' homes clustered in picturesque villages like Port Moresby along the coast. Their simple dwellings, thatched with palm leaves or Kunai grass, were grouped around a ceremonial center place. However, Port Moresby was more of a civilized area than most of the more northern villages because it was a sea port for importing and exporting goods and materials needed for the war effort.

After an overnight rest in Port Moresby, my schedule required starting early for the long over water flight. The restless passengers who were all anxious to have a good time in Sydney boarded my C-47 aircraft. The next stop was 600 miles to a town in the northern part of Australia by the name of Townsville. Townsville was not much more than an outback town having a dirt street down the center with wooden buildings, a bar and bordello with ragged porches and wooden sidewalks, just like you see in American western movies. After refueling and getting ready for another day of flying south, we spent the night in barn-like quarters. For war-weary soldiers this was still not the place to relax and have a good time, so most of the group just had a restless night of drinking the local booze, which was much better than the 190 proof hospital alcohol we drank with grapefruit juice.

The next stop was Brisbane Australia, another 500 miles south along the east coast of Australia. This is the area where the Great Barrier Reef is located off the east coast with the reputation of having an abundance of Great White Sharks. Arriving in Brisbane, it was my first glimpse of civilization since I left San Francisco. It sure looked good. We only stayed there a few hours. While in Brisbane I had my first warm shower in months. It felt wonderful. I stood in the shower for at least an hour. After refueling I took off for the last 400 mile leg to Sydney. Sydney was recognized from the air by all of us as being the first real civilization that we had seen for many months. There was a lot of excitement as we circled for our landing, looking down on the city after months of sleeping in tents in the jungle. We flew around the city before we landed so we could see what it was like. It was a wonderful sight. It looked a lot like Los Angeles. You know, built at all angles. All the roofs were red tile and the city from the air looked like a big fire. After getting a good look at the city we landed at Sydney's municipal field.

We were all thinking, as we looked down at this big city with all its buildings, how we were going to have a good time, especially meeting new girlfriends. We were anxious to find an apartment where we could spend a week, relaxing and touring the town during the day, having fun in the nightclubs, finding attractive girls we could date, eating delicious Australian steak and eggs, and in the evening be able to go to sleep in a clean bed with real sheets and soft pillows.

We checked in at the field and rode a bus into town to report to the leave control center, which was located in the Mark Foys Ltd. Building. Mark Foys was a landmark department store in Sydney that occupied an entire city block. While checking in we could hardly wait to get cleaned up, change clothes, find a date, and see the town. As we were checking in, we met Captain John H. Pennock, our squadron intelligence officer

Captain Pennock's Book

who was in Sydney to publish *The Saga of the Biscuit Bomber,* our squadron's annual.[28] He told us there was a vacant flat in the building where he lived while in Sydney that we could rent for a week. Later we learned that Captain Pennock was stretching his leave in Sydney and might be in serious trouble if he didn't return to Biak soon. I was with a flight officer named Bill Willis who was from our squadron. We said we would take the flat. It was out at Rose Bay. Rose Bay is about 4 miles from the main part of town. The flat was really nice. It had a large bedroom with twin beds, a living room with a radio, a nice kitchen and a tile bathroom.

We cleaned up and went out trolling for cute girls. We went to the Kings Cross to eat. Kings Cross was the night club section of Sydney. We found a restaurant where we had steak and eggs. It sure seemed swell to eat in a restaurant and order anything we wanted. We met a couple of nice girls (I keep telling myself) and went to "Christie's," which was a nightclub. They had a great band, but anything would have sounded good to us at that time. We danced and danced most of the night before returning to our comfortable apartment. Another day we went to Bondi Beach, another favorite tourist spot.

The Australians were friendly to the American flyers but they were suffering from the effects of the war like everyone else. There was limited fuel for automobiles—some of the cars used natural gas, with large balloon-like bladders on the roof of the car for storing the fuel. They were regular cars that had been converted to run on natural gas. There were even some that had wood-burning engines. In spite of this, we were able to take bus tours and taxi rides to see the sights.

The girls didn't think a thing of coming up to our apartment. Young and naïve as I was, I changed my opinion of women after I went to Sydney. The girls we met were fun party girls. I'm not suggesting that they were paid prostitutes, but they liked to drink and dance. In Australia, like the U.S., a lot of men were away in the service, and the women left behind were lonely. We were lonely too, and we had money and nothing to spend it on in New Guinea, so it was natural that we made friends easily. When we had a party in our apartment there would be a lot close dancing that led to petting and fooling around. Some of the older pilots would pair off and find a vacant bedroom. I had listened to the Medical Officer briefings and didn't want to go back to the squad with any STDs, so I restrained myself.

One time we accompanied our chosen girlfriends to dance at an upscale yacht club that one of the girls said was a fun place to visit. There were a lot of large yachts tied up alongside the club. As we partied, someone invited us and our dates to stay over on one of the yachts. As I recall the party group included Willis and all the pilots staying in our apartment. We continued the party onboard. I was still worried about catching something and remained celibate, but confess to a lot of drinking, dancing, and petting. I don't think any of the girls were paid, but they were easily seduced by other pilots from our apartment. It was war time and nobody knew what the future would bring, or even if we had a future. It made everyone behave differently.

We spent three days on the yacht. It was 52 feet long and it sure was a beauty. We went from Rush Cutters Bay at Sydney to Newport and back. It was a wonderful trip. On Saturday we went to the horse races and continued on the lookout for attractive women, someone we could talk to about anything but the war. I really don't care that much for horse races but it was fun, much better than the jungle living conditions we endured during the war. One thing I recall was that the horses went clockwise around the track, opposite to the U.S. practice. Sydney was such a beautiful city I really hated to leave the comforts of civilization and the opportunities for female companionship, but after a while I found I wanted to get back to the war effort and fly dangerous missions.

Sounds crazy, but I really loved to fly!

I had a date every night. I really went wild. I didn't get 2 hours of sleep a night. We kept our apartment in good shape. We bought flowers for the living room and food for the kitchen. We would have our dates cook our dinner when we didn't feel like going out to eat. Let's just say there we had some great parties. I guess you could say we were a wild bunch of Yankee pilots. Unfortunately, the time passed quickly and only too soon I knew I would be flying back to the Philippines and back to the war.

The time in Sydney was very relaxing. It was a comfort to be reminded that there were places in the world where life still continued peacefully, without fighting and fear. Although I went to Sydney to get a rest, it became clear that I'd have to go back to the squadron for my rest!

On the flight back to New Guinea, I was the pilot, but it was a different aircraft, not the one we had come south in. I had some engine problems in a storm over the water between Australia and New Guinea. We were in formation with a second plane. We lost one engine and I had to tell all the passengers to throw out all their equipment and gear, including souvenirs they had bought in Australia, particularly bottles of booze. We also threw out spare equipment from the plane to lighten the load. We barely made it into New Guinea on one engine. The soldiers were always solemn on the flight back to the combat zones, because the time of leave was too short. They hated to go back to crummy food and bad housing, and of course, having to throw away all the goodies they bought in Sydney made it even worse.

When I got back to the outfit, I had twenty letters waiting for me from my Mom—one for every day and then some. There were also packages. I immediately wrote to her and told her about my leave. I closed my letter with "You are the best mother in the world." In hind sight, I was lucky to get to Sydney when I did, because after I returned all leaves were cancelled—permanently.[29]

CHAPTER 14

LIFE IN SAN JOSE: SUPPLYING GUERRILLAS

Our new base at San Jose, Mindoro was in a dry dusty area. Dust blowing across the airstrip was the cause of several accidents. We also had to watch out for the occasional carabao (water buffalo) that wandered across the field. There was a railroad with a small train nearby, also a river. Filipino women washed clothes on the banks of the river, beating them with wooden paddles to get the dirt out. We had some Filipinos working for the squad. Nearby there were farms with fields of corn and rice being cultivated using plows pulled by water buffaloes. We lived in tents by the river, food was field grade, and there were few mosquitoes but millions of flies. I've enjoyed the experience of going different places and seeing how people live. Summing up my experiences, no doubt, the U.S. is best!

Farming with Carabao

After a while our new area was fixed up and became one of the best places our squadron had ever been in and we were settling down for a while. We had an officer's mess and club which were first rate. The Mess Hall was fixed up with parachutes used as a scenic canopy over the room and we had Filipino waiters who even put flowers on the table. Our club was made out of bamboo with a cement floor. The outside roof was covered with *Napa*, which is grass thatching. The sides were covered with *Sawali,* which is a matting made out of something similar to bamboo. We had two new ice boxes, one for the mess hall and one for the club. It would get 120° F in the shade, so those ice boxes were much appreciated. We also had an ice cream machine, and were able to have ice cream once it was running.

Morale was considerably improved, although there was still a lot of griping about the system used for combat leaves. To the pilots, it seemed very uneven. This topic came up repeatedly in the squadron monthly reports, but nothing was ever done to improve it .[30]

There was a barrio (town) near our camp and it had several small restaurants and a few nightclubs. One of the nightclubs had a 12 piece band where we could go and dance with the hostesses, or the local girl entertainers. The girls would also dance and sing for us. This place was very popular because it had the best looking, well-endowed, female entertainers. Some guys would try to line up dates with the girls for later in the evening when they got off work. There was one nice restaurant where we liked to go. It had table clothes on the tables and served good ice cream. Ice cream cost two pesos (one dollar) a cup. That was sort of steep, but when you remember we had never been in a place where we could go to a restaurant, cost didn't matter.

Of course, since we moved, we had to build a new house. I was living with four guys. Bill Willis from Oklahoma, Joe Kennedy from New York, Kenny Milan, from Minnesota and Charlie Reid from LA. They were a swell bunch of guys, all pilots except Charlie, who was a navigator. We'd been building our house very slowly but it was shaping up. We had a Filipino houseboy who was a carpenter and he was doing most of the work. We paid him fifty cents a day. I got a haircut from a Filipino barber for two packs of cigarettes. There were some Filipino girls who cleaned our house and did our laundry. They did a good job, starching and ironing our uniforms. Some of them were not bad looking either—I mean the girls, not the uniforms!

While there I was assigned a mission to deliver food rations to the Philippine guerrillas on a small island (Lubang) in the Philippines. The guerrillas were fighting the Japanese and helping the U.S. win back the

Philippines. All I was told was where this island was geographically located just south of Corregidor, and approximately where a potential landing strip was located. The landing strip was supposed to be near the guerrillas' village of Lubang. They were in critical need of the fresh supplies that were onboard my aircraft.

I took off the next morning from San Jose, Mindoro after getting my morning weather briefing. With my specific verbal orders I flew toward the northwest looking for Lubang. About a half hour before my estimated time of arrival the weather closed in. I had to drop down to a lower altitude, just skimming over the waves, to have any visibility at all. It was mid-May, but the rain was coming down in buckets.[31] The visibility was about ¼ mile. I came upon the island suddenly and had to pull up to clear the trees. We flew around the island just above the trees and couldn't find the strip. The Crew Chief was standing behind me peering out the cockpit window helping me identify things on the ground. We spotted a lot of smashed Jap planes and I knew this strip was somewhere there around those planes and revetments. Finally we saw a grass field inside the peripheral revetments so we made a calculated guess that there must be a runway in between them and decided it was the strip. It was still raining and we could hardly see. I came down over the field several times to look it over. It looked pretty soft and muddy. I had to decide whether to land or not. I put my wheels down, buzzed the area, and bounced the airplane wheels several times to see if the ground was hard enough to land. Remember, that if there was a soft spot and I landed and hit muddy grass on the landing, the aircraft might nose over, causing a total wipeout of airplane and crew. If we survived a crash landing, it probably would take months getting back to my outfit on Mindoro.

Well, the touch and go landing area indicated the surface was hard enough to make a safe landing. I came around with full flaps down, ready to make a short field landing. The copilot and Crew Chief were holding on for dear life. I softly set her down at the end of the open grass area, then the trouble started. Wet grass is as slippery as ice. I started to skid from side to side and when I put the brakes on we would go faster.

We ran off the end of the strip and stopped dead in the mud. The mud was above the hubcaps of the wheels and the props were barely clearing the ground. The plane was unhurt but we couldn't move an inch. I cut the engines and just sat there and cussed for a few minutes. It looked like we were going to be on Lubang for a long time before we could get additional help from Mindoro.

While we were sitting on the grass wondering what to do next the Filipino guerrillas started to pop up around the aircraft from nowhere. Finally the guerilla captain appeared. He was friendly, waving to me as I was looking down from the cockpit. I exited from the plane to meet him. I gave him some secret written orders that I had to deliver and asked his men to unload my airplane. I looked the situation over and it appeared pretty helpless to get out. It was still raining as they unloaded the plane and I thought there was only a slim chance that I might get the airplane in the air again. Scary thoughts of being stranded came to mind.

I told the captain to please put his men to work on digging two ditches that sloped gradually away from the wheels up toward the far end of the strip and line them with bamboo matting (sawali) to improve the ground stability. He gave the order to his men to dig the ramps and unload the supplies from the aircraft. I was worried, however I thought that with the cargo removed and using full power I could get loose and get back into the air. He then asked us if we would be his guests tonight at a party in our honor. He told us that May was the month for festivities on that island. He told us he had fried chicken, carabao milk, wine, tuba, girls, girls, girls etc. I told him that I would like to stay, but I was worried about getting out and would accept his invitation if I could not get the plane out of its mud trap. It was still raining hard and might get worse. The Filipinos were working on digging us out and it looked like it would take about six hours.

I told him we would go to his village, eat lunch with him and come back, and if we couldn't get out then, we would accept his invitation for the party.

He had a carriage, pulled by carabaos, sent out from the village, and we rode into town in style. We met the mayor of the town who was a doctor. He couldn't speak English but seemed very intelligent. The whole town turned out to see us. We entered his house and I was surprised to see how clean it was. He had neat bamboo furniture and the walls were hand-painted. The table was covered with a beautiful tablecloth and clean white napkins were supplied. They treated us like kings and we really had a good time. Some men played a few of their musical instruments and his (the Mayor's) beautiful daughter sang for us. Not bad either. We really enjoyed ourselves and finally had to leave to see if we would be able to take off.

It was still raining and the Filipinos had a hard time digging in the mud. Finally they finished and everything looked all right. I still wasn't sure if we could make it. I walked down the strip, knee deep in the tall grass and looked it over, wondering if I would have enough runway space to get back into the air. In some places it was very soft and I figured out the best direction for a short field take off. I picked out a landmark at the end the grass area to use as a guide, because it was hard to see in the heavy rain storm. The strip was short and the plane would take a while before we could get up to takeoff air speed because the wheels would be buried in the muddy grass. I returned to the aircraft and thanked the guerilla captain and climbed up into the C-47 cockpit, did my preflight checkout and started the engines. I revved up the engines and it seemed to move so we shut down and told the guerilla captain that we were going to give it a try and fly out. He wished us luck and we prepared for a full power short field takeoff. I told the copilot to be ready to drop a quarter flaps at my command.

I opened the throttles to full power and we started slowly to move out of the hole. We were rolling down the grass field on our takeoff run, getting closer to the end of the strip, but still didn't have flying speed. I glanced over and yelled at the copilot to drop a quarter flaps and pull up the gear. We were now airborne and gaining speed a few feet above the ground. Luckily we got off the ground and climbed out, barely missing the trees at the end of the strip. We both looked at each other and smiled. I sure was relieved to get off that island, heading back to Mindoro.[32]

At Elmore Field, San Jose, Mindoro we made the transition to C-46s. This wasn't without problems as we lost three planes in March. One had to ditch in Ormac Bay, but fortunately the entire crew and 30 passengers were rescued by a PT boat. The plane stayed afloat for 15 minutes. I made a point to remember this. That wasn't a long time to get out of the plane, especially with passengers aboard. While we mostly flew the C-46, we still had C-47s for special missions or short fields, as described above. One unusual mission involved fitting two C-47s with tanks and spray nozzles. They were dispatched to fly over Corregidor, over several camps, and over the front lines in various areas around Manila where there were high concentrations of dead enemy casualties. They sprayed these areas with DDT chemicals to disinfect them and kill the swarms of flies that were attracted there. [33]

From Elmore Field we flew a lot of "drop" missions, where we dropped supplies to Army and guerrilla personnel in the field. Other notable events took place as we began to move the Squadron from Mindoro to Porac, a base near Clark Field on Luzon. In preparation for the move (and our return to civilization and close proximity to attractive Filipinas), the Squadron Commander ordered a meeting of all officers. Censorship, radio security, and flight safety were discussed. The meeting ended with Captain Pallone, Medical Officer, giving a lecture on "the physical aspects of sexual relations practices in the Philippines." As I recall, everyone paid close attention. I know I sure did. [34]

We had several more C-46 accidents, only one serious. In that one, the plane had engine trouble, and while attempting to land on a single engine, fell into a dive at 300 feet and crashed into San Pedro Bay, Leyte. I never found out if it stayed afloat or how long, as it didn't matter. The pilot, Andre C. Rembert, and copilot, John C. Kuprock, were killed on impact. These two fatalities brought to nineteen the number of 57th personnel who had died in the line of duty up to that time.

With the move to Luzon imminent, the 375th Group Commander asked for suggestions for a new nickname for the Group. About thirty suggestions were put forth, and the winner was declared to be *"The Tokyo Trolley."* This pretty well typified everyone's sentiment: get to Tokyo so we can get the hell out of here and go home.[35]

CHAPTER 15

LUZON: PORAC AND CLARK FIELD

Our next move was to a base called Porac, north of Manila on the island of Luzon. Our planes were based at Clark Field, close to Porac. From Clark Field we spent a lot of time flying to support the ground troops in northern Luzon (Lingayan Gulf) and then on north towards Japan with men and cargo to support our fighting troops on Okinawa. Again the danger here was another long overwater flight. When you got more than half way to your destination you couldn't turn back and had to keep going to your original destination. Likewise from Okinawa it was roughly the same distance to Tokyo, again over open water.

The first planes into a new airfield would reconnoiter the area and prepare a description of the field, its approaches, length, and other pertinent data. The Squadron had a special form used for this purpose. For example, at Yontan Airfield on Okinawa, where we would soon be flying, the report indicated that the field was approximately one mile inland from the south central coast. The main runway ran northeast-southwest and was level, made of hard graded coral, was 250 feet wide, and 6,800 feet long. The approaches were spelled out through a series of coded locations. No maintenance facilities were available; tents were available at the Marine Transient camp for personnel. Control of the area was

Yontan Airfield Okinawa

by a designated fighter aircraft section, code named "Glacier." Arriving transport aircraft were advised to check in with "Glacier" on frequency 140.58 MHz. The report further advised that foxholes were available in the vicinity of the runway. A siren sounded the alarm, with 5 blasts signaling an airborne invasion; 4 blasts, a possible airborne invasion; 3 blasts, a red alert; and 1 blast, "all clear." Pilots were further advised to avoid Ishigaki and Calayan Islands on their approach to Okinawa, as the Japanese still had medium and heavy anti-aircraft weapons operational on those islands.[36]

Our squadron was fortunate in that most of the Japanese fighter aircraft had been cleared from the areas where we were flying the un-armed C-46s. The only armament we carried was a single Thompson submachine gun that could be fired out the window of the plane. It sounds bad to say this today, but the only time it was used was to shoot at an occasional whale as we flew low over the ocean. There was one occasion in July, as I returned from Okinawa to Luzon, on a C-46 flight with Lt. Craig Headley, when we sighted a Japanese "Betty" type 1 me-dium bomber flying on a heading of 135 degrees (southeast) toward us on our starboard side. The Tommy gun would have been no help against the heavily armed bomber. I was worried that if they spotted us they would attack, so I made a quick evasive decision. I could not see an approaching aircraft back underneath my airplane so to reduce the chance of the bomber coming in low behind us I immediately dove the aircraft down to sea level, flying just a few feet above the whitecaps for the last several hundred miles towards Lingayan Gulf on Luzon to avoid the bomber. The Japanese pilot appar-ently did not see us or he

Lingayan Gulf Airstrip

needed to complete his original mission. The bomber was soon lost to sight in the overcast. We never knew what happened to the Japanese aircraft after that.[37]

During April and May I was very busy flying supplies up and down the Philippine Islands, or running back to Peleliu or Biak to bring in new supplies or evacuate wounded. I had progressed to the point where I was flying as 1st pilot one hundred percent of the time.

While our Squadron 57 administrative operations were at Porac Airfield in Luzon, just south of Clark Field, the C-47 and C-46 aircraft operations were housed at Clark Field. Clark was a convenient location for mission staging and loading even though mission planning was

Clark Field 1945

initiated at Porac. The flying operations from Clark primarily were to carry cargo to and from Okinawa and Biak Island. I also flew a number of training flights for the new pilots, making numerous C-47 overnight flights to Porac Field. Porac was heavily used by a 5th Air Force P-47D "Thunderbolt" fighter group that was supporting ground troops that were still fighting in northern Luzon.

While spending my leisure time at Porac, I met some of the P-47

"Thunderbolt" fighter pilots while spending hours playing poker. In between telling war stories and playing poker, I made an unofficial agreement with one of the P-47 pilots. I would check him out in flying my C-46 if he would let me fly his P-47 solo around the landing pattern. The P-47 was challenging because it was the heaviest fighter bomber. We traded flight operation manuals and over a couple of weeks read all the information about each other's aircraft. I was lucky because the two radial

P-47s, Floridablanca

engines of the C-46 were the same engine used in the single engine P-47 Thunderbird fighter. So I had some knowledge of how to control the P-47 engine and propeller. My friend had it a little easier because I would be his co-pilot as he flew the C-46 around the Porac flight pattern. The P-47 squadron was based at nearby Floridablanca airfield. After getting familiar with the P-47 cockpit instruments and controls, I practiced taxiing around the field and getting familiar with the flight controls. I decided that I could make it around the pattern and land this high performance aircraft without crashing.

Take off at full power was a little tricky because of the high engine torque and limited rudder control. I made it off the ground with trepidation, climbing up to the pattern level 1,000 feet above the field, so far so good on the downwind leg. I left the landing gear in the down position. I decided not to retract the gear so I could concentrate on the flight controls. As I turned on the base leg, I was worried about knowing the stall speed limits of the P-47 that would be critical on the final approach. Now came the most dangerous part of this solo flight. The radial engine was blocking the front view from the cockpit so you could not see straight ahead. As I turned onto the final approach from the base leg I had to do it slowly and not be aligned with the runway until I passed over the runway markings so I could view the runway from the side window, only lining up with the runway at the last instant while watching my critical air speed and setting up a stall just as my wheels touched down.

Pheeew! The roll down the runway commanded all my attention, keeping the aircraft on the center line as I slowed down and used brakes for direction control. I returned the aircraft to my friend as I climbed out of the cockpit with a smile on my face. The ground crew then breathed easier. I had renewed admiration for the pilots that flew these planes while engaging enemy pilots in acrobatics.

June 6th was another important day for me, as I got my First Lieutenant's silver bars. I celebrated that night with some of the other pilots and crewmen. One of the guys had just come back from Sydney and he had a lot of Aussie beer and whiskey. Kibbe contributed three cases of Cokes. Later I heard it was a great party. I don't remember a lot because I passed out at 2:00 A.M. In hindsight I'm not proud of the drinking, but it was a way to forget for a few hours the stress, danger, and loneliness we felt. We never drank before a mission, however.

Around this time I got a telephone call from my best friend Cliff. I had flown a C-47 to Porac for training. While there, I received a phone call from the Army Signal Corps that a friend of mine named Fred Clifford was trying to contact me. The Army telephone system was pieced together via code names. When you used the phone you set up a ring. The next switching station would respond that it was "Mountain View" (or some code name) and did you want to go to "Park" (code for Manila) or some other location. I finally contacted Cliff's merchant marine ship at a dock south of Manila. I had some training to finish so I told Cliff to hitch hike up to Clark Field and where he could find me. We got together and went bar-hopping in Manila for a night of catching up on each other's escapades. When it was time to return to his ship, I took a C-47 for local training and I flew him back. It turned out there was a dirt strip right by his boat. It was quite a sight for his shipmates to see a C-47 come roaring out of the sky, land there,

Cliff & Bob, Clark Field

and a single passenger exit, namely Cliff, looking like he was a three-star General or some other big-wig. You can bet I buzzed that ship after I took off from that dirt strip. I did not see Cliff again until I returned home at the end of the war. Our coded map had worked for a second time!

We made lots of trips from Clark Field to Okinawa delivering badly needed supplies for the invasion of the Japanese homeland. On one of these trips I had what potentially could have been a fatal accident. On July 17th I took off with a full load that consisted of two 2000-pound bombs. I had to crawl over the bombs to get into the cockpit. After taxing out to the runway and completing my preflight checks for a morning takeoff to Okinawa, with approval from the control tower I set full throttle for takeoff. I started down the foggy runway, ready to climb up into the low clouds just above the runway where I would have to totally rely on my instruments. Halfway down the runway I noticed that my airspeed instrument was not working. I didn't have any indication of airspeed, and I was taking off into bad weather. Without knowing airspeed, there was no way we were going to survive. We had two airspeed meters, one for the pilot one for the copilot. I could not see the copilot's airspeed indicator well enough to fly on instruments. At this point I did the only thing possible, which was to pull back the throttles, stand on the brakes, and hope for the best. The plane was fully loaded and almost at flying speed, which made it very difficult to stop. I lost control of the airplane as it veered off the runway, went down into a gulley and up the other side over a small mound of dirt, and onto a taxiway on another part of the field. The taxiway was loaded with other aircraft and my C-46D left wing hit the wing one of the parked planes, a B-24 bomber. We collided wing tip to wing tip, damaging both planes as mine slowly rolled to a stop. Other than that, we came out okay.[38]

Following the incident we had a review, but I never did figure out what the problem was until years later when I read the accident report found in the Air Force archives. As part of a preflight check out, the pilot has to go around and remove the protective covers from the pitot tubes that supply air pressure to the airspeed indicating devices. I was certain that I had done this, so it must've been some other problem.

The accident report said that the pitot valve feeding the two airspeed indicators malfunctioned only on the pilot's side. Meanwhile, until the review board reached a conclusion, I was grounded.

The review board met and published their report the next day. When the accident review was completed, I was exonerated.

Five days later I was put back on first pilot status and became very busy, flying both C-47s and C-46s and also instructing new pilots. I would take up some of the new pilots and show them a few things that would help their flying, then I'd let them make some landings and takeoffs. Looking back, it's a wonder I'm still alive. They bounced that airplane so much I was almost sure it would fall apart. It was really a sweat job. I can't remember if I was that bad during training, but I probably was! I remember when I first got in the squadron and they used to take me up for instruction. I would just dream of the day when I would be the one who was pilot. You have a lot of responsibility. As pilot, you are responsible for the lives of the four men in the crew and sometimes as many as 40 passengers.

It was really funny sometimes when I was carrying a load of personnel and made a rough landing. They all looked as if they would walk rather than fly the next thousand miles. Of course, I knew it wasn't funny to them. We just got hardened to having to land in rough weather.

Army WACS

One time I was carrying a load of WACs and a Colonel came running out to the plane and wanted to ride. Well, we were having a lot of fun with the WACs and I didn't want him to ride and put a damper on the party, so I said "Sure you can go." Then I turned to the copilot and I said "Boy, that last landing was a son of a bitch, I thought we'd all be killed. Look at that weather coming in, we'll never make it out of here." After a while of this the Colonel finally piped up and said "Oh

I forgot, there is a friend of mine I want to see." He practically broke into a run getting away from the plane.

For a while I considered staying over in the Army Air Force so I could get promoted, get my captaincy, but decided I'd rather go home than remain overseas an extra five months or whatever it took. At the time, I thought I only had four more months to go and I was eligible to go home. So far everybody had been going home as per schedule, once their rotation had been approved. Some of the older pilots had been overseas for at least two years, maybe more. The thing that was so frustrating was that there was no clear definition of what it took. If the rules didn't change, I thought I could make it home for next Christmas. One thing good about those days was that time just seemed to pass so fast.

I wrote a lot of letters home to my Mother so she wouldn't worry about me and to thank her for all her letters and packages. Sometimes I had missions that lasted four or five days and then I couldn't write. Meanwhile my brother Jack got married and my sister had a new boyfriend. I was missing out on a lot of changes at home.

On the other hand, conditions were improving in Porac. The food at the new base was excellent. On a typical night we had fried chicken, corn on the cob (one of my favorites) dressing, iced tea, ice water, fresh butter, bread, fruit salad, raspberry ice cream. There were times when I thought I was going to hate to leave this overseas duty. But then I'd hear from home and know that I wanted to get back to be with the family once again. I did miss home very much and wanted to return.

On July Fourth we threw a party at the WAC detachment. I had a cute little girl friend there and I would try to see her every night when I wasn't flying. We'd go dancing and eat in small Filipino cafés. She was 24 years old, but only looked about 20, so I wasn't bothered about being younger. We weren't serious, just good friends enjoying each other's company. It was hard to make personal commitments at those times, when either one of us could find ourselves suddenly transferred with no opportunity to see each other again.[39]

Flying over Nakagusku Bay Okinawa

On flights from Clark field to Okinawa, we typically had bad weather. One time I tried three times and each time was turned back, until I finally made it through on the fourth try. After landing in Okinawa, I learned that I was the first plane there in more than a week. A Colonel came running out from control and commandeered my plane to fly to a new airstrip in northern Okinawa. I said, "Okay, jump in and we'll go. You know where it is, right?"

When we got there, the airfield was under construction. There were bulldozers and scrapers working on the runway, which was not finished. The Colonel ordered me to land anyway. I buzzed the field a couple of times until the construction guys got the idea and moved all the heavy equipment down to the end of the runway. When I landed the plane put ruts in the newly laid gravel sub base the ground crew had been placing. The Colonel in charge of the field was roaring mad and came out to the plane to chew me out, but I told him I had orders and turned him over to my Colonel so they could fight it out among themselves. As soon as they were away from the plane I jumped back on board. Meanwhile the construction crew was starting back at work on the field and didn't want to move, so I gunned the engines as part of my takeoff engine tests sitting on the newly graded strip, hoping the construction crew would get clear. As I roared down the field straight at them I lifted off right over the heads of the equipment operators. When the plane passed overhead with engines screaming, they raised their fingers in a friendly obscene gesture.

As the flights to Okinawa became more frequent, we were briefed on emergency procedures. In the case of having to ditch at sea, we were given instructions on radio communications and also provided with additional emergency equipment for each plane, including Chinese identifications, Chinese money, and trading materials. We had heard enough about Japanese atrocities—especially their treatment of fliers— that we did not want to find ourselves as POWs.

I discovered later, it was only three months after my briefing, that in October 1945, a Navy destroyer sailed into Chichi Jima (an island near Iwo Jima), to disarm the Japanese soldiers there and repatriate them to Japan. It was one of the war's most horrific atrocities that was uncovered. Six American fliers whose planes had been shot down were held as POWs for a while on the island and then executed. The livers and flesh of several were eaten by their Japanese captors.[40] Former U.S. President George H. W. Bush narrowly escaped a similar fate. His carrier-based fighter bomber was shot down in the same area. (There was a high powered radio transmitting station on a peak on Chichi Jima the fliers were trying to destroy). He parachuted into the sea and was seen by the Japanese on the island. He got into his life raft, but the wind and current were carrying him back towards the island. He had no oars, so he paddled with his hands in the opposite direction. He had the good luck to be rescued by a nearby submarine.[41]

On July 26, I had a long 7 hour flight from Luzon to Ie Shima Island and back the next day. Ie Shima is one of the outlying islands near the northwest end of Okinawa. During the next few months I made several trips there. Looking back, it made me sad when I realized that was where Ernie Pyle, the much beloved and famous WWII war correspondent, was killed on April 18, 1945. He was very popular among all the troops for his courage and sense of humor.

Ie Shima Island

PART IV

MOVE TO OKINAWA•JAPAN SURRENDERS AFTER HIROSHIMA AND NAGASAKI•FIRST FLIGHTS INTO TOKYO•NEW BASE:TACHIKAWA, NEAR TOKYO•JAPAN EARLY DAYS OF OCCUPATION.

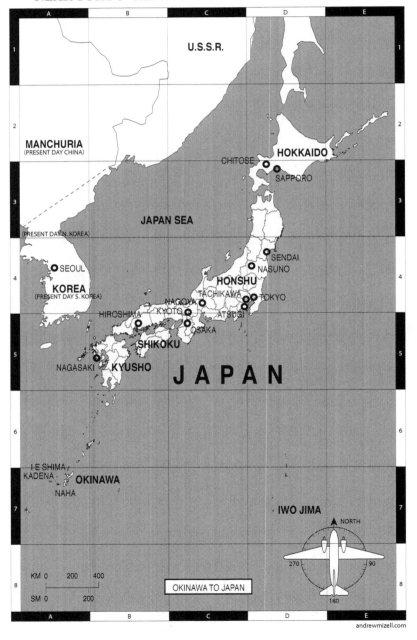

andrewmizell.com

CHAPTER 16

OKINAWA: JAPAN SURRENDERS

From Okinawa we were preparing to invade the Japanese mainland. Military planners had developed an invasion plan known as "Operation Downfall." It consisted of two parts. *Operation Olympic* was intended to invade and capture the southern area of Kyushu, while *Operation Coronet* was the invasion of the Kanto Plain, on Honshu, near Tokyo. The idea was that airbases captured on Kyushu in *Operation Olympic* would provide air cover for *Operation Coronet*. The shortcoming of these plans was that the Japanese knew where the Allied Forces would land, since these were the only coastal locations where amphibious landings were feasible. The Japanese developed defensive plans aimed at repelling invaders from these same locations. The Allied plans were made before the existence of the atomic bomb was known. There were various estimates of the expected casualties, ranging from 100,000 Allied fatalities to as many as half a million, with millions wounded. Japanese fatalities were projected to be as high as five to ten million, many of them untrained civilian conscripts who would be swept into defending the homeland. Use of the atomic bombs, as horrible as they were, undoubtedly saved millions of Allied troops, tens of thousands of Allied POWs held in Japan and elsewhere in Asia, and millions of Japanese civilians who otherwise would have been caught up in the fighting.

We did not know this in July and August, 1945. What we knew was that Okinawa was the staging area where the Allied forces were preparing for the final thrust forward to Japan. The Navy was bringing in all their ships, men, and supplies, for hopefully the last big campaign of the Pacific War. We anticipated that we soon would be flying to Japan in support of the invasion

There was no emergency landing place between Okinawa and Tokyo, but the Navy had stationed submarines at certain locations in the case planes had to ditch in the ocean. Fortunately I never had to do this, but we were always in communication by radio with the submarines somewhere down in the ocean beneath us. I could look down and see the submarines as we passed over them. It gave me a nice feeling that I had a potential rescue team close by just in case. We would contact the submarines over our radio and joke about how much better it was to be in our aircraft rather than in a submarine, especially when we had nurses aboard. They would jokingly respond saying that if we hot pilots lost an engine, they would be there to pull us out of the drink. Sadly, when we were briefed on these over water flights, we would be told to keep our eye out in a certain area for planes that had gone down. Unfortunately I never found any planes or crew. With all of the flying we did you got tuned into the engines. By listening to the engines I could always tell almost immediately if something wasn't right.

While on Okinawa I visited towns that were close to our airfields. There was terrible devastation on Okinawa. We had little interaction with the Okinawans, although some worked at the field, loading and unloading aircraft. I can remember being at Kadena airfield, when a big typhoon hit. When the wind started blowing from one direction we

Kadena Airfield, Okinawa

tried to prop up our tents and footlockers and other belongings so they wouldn't blow away. Then, after the typhoon center passed overhead, the wind came from the other direction and flattened everything anyway.

The end of the war came suddenly on August 15, 1945 (August 14, U.S. time), after the atomic bombing of Nagasaki. At the time I was at the Naha airfield on Okinawa. We had been subject to periodic kamikaze attacks, particularly on all the ships staging at Okinawa close to the Naha sandy beach. In fact, on August 14, the night before the surrender, we all took shelter when Japanese planes came over and destroyed several of our planes on the ground. At the time of the surrender, censorship rules

Naha, the Main City on Okinawa, Wiped-Out after the Fighting

were still in effect. I wrote a brief letter home to my mother telling her about our surprise when we learned about the atomic bomb and then how sudden the news of the Japanese surrender was to all of us. I also mentioned briefly that there'd been a big firework show when we learned of the surrender. However, due to censorship, all I could say was that I was in a "forward area." I closed by saying that everything was going crazy, I couldn't say what we were doing, but I did say that I'd only had four hours sleep in the last three days because of how busy we were. I flew on 20 days in August, nearly 100 hours in the air, mostly long 6 and

7 hour flights back and forth from the Philippines to Okinawa.[42]

A few weeks later, censorship was lifted, and on September 8, 1945 I wrote the following letter to my mother, describing the events that occurred when the surrender was announced.

Dear Mom:

I received several letters from you telling me about all the celebrations for V-J day in the States. I told you in one of my letters that I was in a forward area (it was Okinawa) when the Japanese gave up. I was sleeping alone under my plane when I heard the act-ack (antiaircraft weapons) start firing. I heard everybody yelling and screaming. It scared me half to death. I thought the Japanese had made a landing were trying to take back Okinawa. I was finally brought out of the dark by the Crew Chief. When he told me, I took it as a joke, but sure enough it was the truth.

That night on Okinawa I saw the most spectacular show I've ever seen in my life. It was beautiful. Every gun on Okinawa was being fired. Tracer bullets were covering the sky, shells were exploding, making the night seem like day. Radio Okinawa was telling everybody to stay off the roads and stay in their camps. Everybody was intoxicated with excitement, or maybe just intoxicated. The infantry boys were the ones who were celebrating the most. I don't blame them. They're the ones who've been doing the fighting and taking everything on the chin.

Of course, we were happy too. We took our flare guns and shot red, yellow, blue, green, and white flares into the air. It was beautiful. It's a wonder that nobody got hurt. Everybody was firing their guns. Machine guns, pistols, carbines, you name it. The act-ack put on a real show, it made you seem empty inside when we saw all the ack ack open up. Just the night before, everybody hit the dirt when the Japanese came over. They knocked out several of our airplanes, literally just the night before.

When I got back to Fort Stotsenberg at Clark Field, everybody had been celebrating and were still going strong. The nurses held an open house, the WACS had parties, and the Fort Stotsenberg officers club was having a dance every night and if you think we didn't celebrate, try again!

I'm now flying at 7,000 feet at 180 mph going towards Tachikawa. It is an airfield on the outskirts of Tokyo. Our squadron has been flying to Tokyo frequently since August 29. I was not on the first flight in because we only sent two airplanes. In all, we sent 10 airplanes from the 375th group. All of our planes now have "Tokyo Trolley" painted on the sides. There were news pictures taken so maybe you'll be able to see some of our planes.

The Japanese don't say much. They salute everybody, but they don't smile. We just stare at them and they just stare at us. I haven't seen much of Tokyo yet. All that I've seen is just from the air. It looks like we've finally hit civilization. We were restricted to the shadow of the airplane so I can't tell very much about the people and customs yet. The ones that unloaded the plane were intelligent. They are pretty well organized and could have fought for quite a while longer. The Japanese officers were all dressed up in their best uniforms. They all carry swords and you would be surprised how many wear horn rim glasses. Some of our planes are flying over to Manchuria. I haven't been there yet but I will tell you about it when I go. After this trip to Japan, I will tell you more about it also.

We're now living on Okinawa and have been for some time. We're supposed to move to the Tokyo area as soon as we get everybody else moved up. MacArthur is putting on a show, sending everything in by air so we are the ones who are really working hard now. I still love my work. I have over 1000 flying hours now. I don't know about my captaincy yet. Everything is in such a turmoil. Half of our squadron is going home on points. As yet, I don't have a chance. I only have around 73 points. If rotation on time overseas doesn't change, I should be home for next Christmas.

Take care of yourself. I'm perfect in all respects.
Your loving son, Bob
PS censorship has been lifted, so now I can tell you what we've been doing. [43]

Following that first exciting flight into "Enemy Territory," the ***Tokyo Trolley*** really got moving. We had flights going every day to Tachikawa or Atsugi airports near Tokyo. Once the surrender was announced, everyone's thoughts turned to going home. The Army announced various plans for establishing priority for who got to go. One scheme was based on how many "points" pilots had accumulated, based on hours of flying time and participation in various missions. The other method was based on "rotation," which was linked to total time served overseas. I had originally put in for permission to go home based on the rotation system. Later I had enough points, but they didn't like you to change systems, once you had applied. My situation was further complicated by the fact that I was considering applying for promotion to captain. If I was accepted for my captaincy, it would mean a commitment to remain longer overseas. Torn between this and the desire to go home, I kept wavering about making the decision. Later some events occurred which made me unhappy with the change in command, now that the war was over, and I firmly resolved to get home as soon as possible. I optimistically hoped that this might be in time for Christmas, but events dragged on and it soon became clear I would not make it home until sometime early in 1946.

CHAPTER 17

FIRST FLIGHT TO TOKYO

After the surrender we moved the squadron to Japan and eventually we were based at Tachikawa Airfield outside Tokyo. I stayed in Japan for about four months, from September 1945 through Christmas, and until January 1946. During those first chaotic days after the surrender we really didn't know what to expect when we landed in Japan.

After the peace was declared we first flew into Atsugi airfield near Tokyo, the first Japanese airport we landed at. There was no planning, no briefings that I can recall. As I remember, early one morning somebody called in and said: "Mosier, get up you are going to Tokyo." One C-46 from the 57th was allowed to be among the first planes to land

Hiroshima in Ruins.

there. That was a different pilot; I was not amongst the first to go. Thus, on August 31, 1945, *The Tokyo Trolley* completed its line and reached the end station![44] Atsugi airport was south of Tokyo. When we landed I saw that the Russians were already there. There was a bunch of Russian PBYs lined up along the runway. However, we were greeted by an American officer who had landed first. We unloaded troops there and later drove in a jeep into Tokyo. At the first chance I got I flew over Nagasaki and Hiroshima. In Nagasaki the town was in a valley. It was totally demolished and all trees that had been growing on the hillsides of the valley were blown flat, laying there like so many telephone poles. In Hiroshima only fireplaces were standing and in some places metal safes could be seen. Otherwise, everything else was flattened, except for a few concrete structures in the middle of the town.

Commencing in August when we got busy flying supplies to Okinawa from the Philippines, and then later when we were flying to Japan, there was more night flying. In the cockpit at night our instrumentation lights were dimmed and red to maintain our night vision. There were times when flying at night was beautiful, when the night sky was illuminated by the stars and moon and we could see the ocean below in the moonlight. On other nights, with clouds or stormy weather, we could see very little and had to rely upon our instruments. As pilot I had to keep an eye on the critical gages, those that monitored the engine temperatures, rpm's, and the cylinder head pressures. This was critical—if the pressure got too high we had to change the flight parameters. Of course, we had to keep our eye on fuel consumption, and from time to time manually balance the fuel flow from different tanks to maintain the aircraft's trim. We carried snacks and had little immersion heaters that we could put in a cup of water and make coffee or tea.

Night flying was difficult because the landing areas typically had few lights, so we essentially made a guess using the ADF (automatic direction finder) to locate the runway. After the Japanese surrendered, we had better equipment for landings. The Air Force brought in two trailers of equipment for making Ground Controlled Approaches (GCA) and installed them at our two main Japanese airports, the Okinawa airports and Clark Field. One trailer had ground radar that tracked the incoming aircraft in the landing pattern. The second trailer held the radar displays and communications systems where the ground controller could talk to the pilot and give him feedback about his approach. The ground controller would describe our glide slope and tell us over the radio, if we were on the proper glide slope. When we were on final approach, they would advise if we were lined up properly right and left.

When not flying, we pilots went into Tokyo to look around, always carrying our 45s, but we never had any problems with the Japanese. When the Emperor told the Japanese that the war was over, the war was over. We kept very busy getting troops and supplies in for the occupation. This was before the formal surrender was signed on September 2, 1945.

The Japanese people demonstrated their resiliency in many ways. When the Emperor told them to " … endure the unavoidable and suffer what is unsufferable…" they did it. Perhaps we weren't accepted, but we were tolerated. As the occupation took effect and the number of Allied personnel in Japan grew, the Japanese rebounded, making souvenirs that would appeal to the foreigners. We could buy American flags and other western items that certainly had not been made previously in Japan.

While in Japan I flew a lot of missions around to different areas. What I liked best was helping people, taking supplies in where they were needed or taking the wounded back so that they could receive prompt medical treatment. Unfortunately I never got a lot of details about the people we helped. I might see them briefly when they came on board but then all my attention had to be focused on flying the airplane and I didn't really get a chance to know much about the passengers.

Video of first landing at Atsugi can be found at:

https://www.youtube.com/watch?v=TyswklkPlM4

The letter following the k and the P is an "ell," not a "one."

CHAPTER 18

HOKKAIDO RESCUE:
WE "CAPTURE" AN AIRFIELD

After the peace treaty was signed on September 2, 1945 we were busy flying missions carrying troops and supplies between Okinawa and Japan. In mid-September several planes from our squad had a mission to fly to Atsugi airport in Japan and back to Okinawa. When we first arrived at Atsugi, we were told they needed some aircrafts to fly north to the island of Hokkaido, where we were to pick up some allied POWs who'd been held there for over three years.[45]

Later I learned that there were four main POW camps in the southern section of Hokkaido, centered around the town of Sapporo. These camps together held more than 1,000 allied POWs, a mixture of British, Americans, and Dutch. Some of the Americans had been captured on Wake Island, early in the war. During their period of captivity, many of the POWs were moved several times from one work site to another. POWs were forced to do a variety of jobs, many working as slave laborers in the coal mines of the Hokkaido Shipping and Mining Company Ltd. and Sumitomo Mining Company.[46]

The first day we started out we ran into some weather and had to turn around and come back to Atsugi. The next day, September 15th, we made it, with the weather being beautiful all the way north.[47] It was an opportunity to see a new part of Japan, and Hokkaido was the farthest north that I had been, with latitude about the same as Portland Oregon. The field where we landed was at Chitose, where there was a Japanese

Navy Air Corps school. The Japanese were still doing calisthenics and drills near the field. It reminded me of when I was a cadet. We had to get refueled there and the only way they could refuel the plane was with 50 gallon drums of aviation gasoline using hand pumps. We watched the refueling process to make sure it was done properly and the fuel was okay. Then the Japanese took us to the POWs officers' mess where we were fed. Lunch consisted mostly of American rations, but also with some Japanese bread and butter and tangerines.

We had 32 POWs put on each of our three planes. At this point the prisoners were in pretty good shape. They'd been fed and they'd been issued new clothes and the main thing they wanted was just to get the hell out of there. The POWs on my plane were all British. Once loaded, we took off and flew back south. When we were about 200 miles north of Tokyo, the weather started to close in. When the war was on we used a code for weather. SAVANNA meant weather. SAVANNA ONE was good weather and SAVANNA FIVE was closed in, very bad weather. Tokyo was SAVANNA FIVE, closed, and we didn't have enough fuel to go back or to fly around waiting for the weather to clear. We went down low and the bad weather was right down to the ground. Fortunately we spotted a Japanese dirt strip about 150 miles north of Tokyo. I decided to land there. We didn't know whether the Japanese would be friendly or not, but there was nothing else we could do so we landed. There were a lot of Japanese medium bombers on the field. When we landed our airplane sunk down in the dirt, not too much, just enough to slow us down. The Japanese didn't build strips for heavy aircraft. Our C-46's weighed 43,000 pounds loaded.

All three of our planes taxied up to the end of the strip and stopped. We did not want to taxi off the strip for fear of getting stuck for good. We cut our engines and everybody got out. There were approximately 100 men, counting the POWs. As we looked around, the place looked deserted. Finally we spotted one lone Japanese coming across the field.

He got about halfway across when he stopped and took off his sword and stuck it in the ground. He must have been pretty brave to come across the field with about 100 men waiting for him. We were the first Americans in to that field. I spoke with the POWs and found one man who was fluent in Japanese, and with him and a couple of other men I started out to meet the Japanese, who was waiting some distance away. He was very militaristic and proper. He walked at attention all way to meet us. When he got within speaking distance, about 200 feet away, he stopped and gave a snappy salute, which we returned. He indicated he was ready to surrender to us. Our interpreter could speak very good Japanese because he had been a prisoner for 3 ½ years. Through him we learned that the Japanese was a Captain.

From our charts, we knew where we were, but this field was not on the map and we wanted to know the name of the field, its length, and so on. We also asked if he was in command of the field. As translated, in so many words the Japanese Captain replied, "No, I'm the big cheese at this end of the field, but there's a bigger cheese at the other end." He was really nervous and I don't blame him because there were over 90 POWs standing nearby that did not have much love for the Japanese. As we looked over our maps he was shaking so much he couldn't even point to where we were. Finally the "bigger cheese" came out of hiding. He came across the field in a car waving a white flag. He was a major. He got out of the car but was scared to walk up to us until the Japanese Captain told him we landed, not to capture them, but just because of weather. The major finally came up and he and the Captain went through all the bowing ceremonies and everything that goes with Japanese military courtesy. Finally we learned that we were at Nasuno Airfield in Togchi Prefecture, north of Tokyo.

They asked us if we planned on staying all night and we said yes, if the weather didn't clear up. The major asked us if we could eat Japanese rice and we said we would try anything once, so he sent out a runner to heat up 500 pounds of rice. He really overestimated the American appetite because that was 5 pounds per man. He got cars out to take us over to their barracks but by then the weather cleared up. We knew they were expecting us at Atsugi and if we didn't show up they would probably send out a search party for us. So we left without eating the rice. I really would not have felt safe staying there at night anyway. Besides, our POWs were very anxious to get to Tokyo and find transport where they could finally make their way home. They had had enough of Japan.

To continue, I'll describe a typical day in the life of a troop carrier pilot during those hectic times. After returning from Hokkaido, early the next morning we got up to fly south back to Okinawa, but there was a typhoon on course towards Japan that would keep us grounded 48 hours or more, so we decided to go into Yokohama and Tokyo. We hitchhiked into Yokohama and looked around. It was really bombed out. The people were living in shantytowns built out of scrap. There were quite a few nice buildings left, but MacArthur had taken them over for headquarters. After we looked around a while we took an electric train to Tokyo. Surprisingly the Japanese transportation system was still operating pretty well. They had regular streetcars, elevated railroads and subways. We didn't have to pay a thing, we just got on and rode.

We looked all around Tokyo, which was in better shape than Yokohama. The Japanese people seemed glad the war was over. So far, not one American had been hurt by the Japanese. They just go on as if there was never was a war. We didn't even carry a gun with us on that trip. We found a very nice hotel to stay at, called the Marunouchi hotel, located just a little distance away from the Imperial Hotel. The rooms were really nice, clean sheets and pillow cases, three-quarter beds with innerspring mattresses. The rooms had hot and cold running water and cost ¥10 a day, which was about $.70. We ate supper there and breakfast at the hotel the next morning. The meals cost ¥9 which was about $.63. I didn't much care for the food. Everything they cooked smelled like fish and tasted just as bad, including their steak.

After touring Tokyo, I came back to our base at Atsugi, where I found myself living on the airplane and eating C rations, waiting for a big typhoon to blow over. Sitting on the plane, I was writing a letter to my mother to tell her about these latest adventures. The wind was so strong it was making it hard to write with the plane bouncing around like a boat. At one point, I thought the airplane was going to blow away.

When the weather calmed down and I flew back to Okinawa, the base had been hit hard. Our tent there had been leveled by the typhoon. I had to search around through the wreckage to try to find what was left of my belongings.

CHAPTER 19

TACHIKAWA, JAPAN

Our next move was to Tachikawa field, located about 11 miles from the Imperial Palace. This was the "Wright Field" of Japan. Runways were not designed for the heavier landing loads of our planes, and sometimes they broke through the concrete. After landing, when we weren't flying, we had a chance to look around. The buildings were deserted. Going through the buildings we could see where the Japanese did their research and designed and tested aircraft. The wind tunnels were there, along with a lot of other equipment, such as calculators, slide rules, and other stuff. They had perfect models of our aircraft and parts. We slept in a hangar, which had glass skylights, with much of the glass blown out. It rained a lot and water came into the buildings, so we had to locate our cots in the dry spots. We had to stay in the hangers until we got the office buildings cleaned up so we could live in them. It was very cold there and we had no hot water showers. The showers were outdoors and ice cold.[48]

While here, I did a lot of flying. I spent my 21st birthday shuttling between Tachikawa and Atsugi airports. There were a lot of personnel changes going on, putting new men into our squadron, and sending the older guys home. I became flight leader and decided I would stay over after all so I could get promoted to Captain. I wrote home to tell my mother of my decision, but I also told her that if I had to sign anything saying I'd agree to stay overseas longer than usual, I would turn it down. If everything ran smoothly, I thought I'd get my captaincy about the first of December 1945. Everything was so mixed up at that time I couldn't be sure about anything. A lot of men were going home on points except flying officers. There was a chance I could get sent home on points, because I had (or thought I had) 75 points, based on my seven battle stars.

We were still living in the large hanger that leaked and it was raining all the time when I was informed that I was now Assistant Operations Officer. At this time I still didn't know when I would get to go home, and I was still thinking about going for my Captaincy. I learned that Kibbe and Headley, two fellows I came overseas with, were on their way home. It was hard for me to stay in Japan while they got to go home. I checked and found that I had 72 points towards going home. Not quite enough![49]

While I was in Japan, Okinawa got hit again by a bad typhoon. The first really disastrous typhoon was *Typhoon Cobra*, Dec 14-19, 1944. This inflicted more damage on the American Navy in the vicinity of Okinawa than the Japanese had ever been able to do. It is sometimes referred to as Halsey's Typhoon.[50] The second was *Typhoon Louise* which struck Okinawa October 9, 1945 and flattened many ground facilities and damaged ships and facilities in south Okinawa at Buckner Bay. It sank 22 ships and grounded hundreds of others, then went on to hit Japan. I went back to Okinawa after completing some missions in Japan. Everything on Okinawa was torn up. All the tents were knocked down—the typhoon had made a direct hit on Okinawa.

It continued to be very cold. I was assigned some instructing duties because we were short of 1st Pilots. Riding in the copilot's seat got very tiresome. One day I flew down to Atsugi to gas up a plane. There I met one of the other pilots, Joe Kennedy who was executive officer in our squadron. We decided to fly formation back to Tachikawa. When we came back to land, we were told to hold at 1,000 feet because some Navy Corsairs were coming in for landing and they had priority. Kennedy and I called the tower and asked permission to buzz the tower and make a peel off into the pattern after the Navy landed. We were given permission. We buzzed the tower and using the C-46 trim tab wheel, we went up at an 85% angle and did a loop up and around. At the top of the loop I put the gear down and greased in the landing. We really made a good job of it. As I came roaring down towards the runway with Joe Kennedy's C-46 following close behind, I passed directly over a Jeep stopped at the end of the runway. I didn't realize it at the time, but that Jeep belonged to General Olds. He was the big shot there at that time.

When we got back from lunch a message came through for Mosier, Mouche, Kennedy, and Kirkling to report to General Olds. This was us two pilots and our copilots, so we figured we were in trouble. We had not shaved for several days and were pretty scrubby looking, so we had to clean up fast and then reported in at 2 o'clock. The General asked us "What were you trying to do, be fighter pilots?" He asked how long we'd been overseas, how much time we had in the airplanes, whether we were unloaded or loaded, etc. Luckily we had no passengers other than crew. He never gave us a chance to say a word other than "Yes," or "No." He said that he had never seen a transport plane make such a steep peel off and he was going to recommend to Colonel Roth our new commanding officer that we should fly copilot the rest of our time overseas.

Then he kicked us out of his office. The only thing we worried about was that maybe Colonel Roth would have us court-martialed. If we just got off with being copilots, we figured we'd be lucky. I was mad because we'd been doing this kind of flying throughout the war and in some cases even riskier maneuvers to get into tight places and now we had some new commanding officers just over from the States and they were trying to change everything. We didn't have the slightest idea that we were doing anything wrong except a little sharp flying. The thing was that we were Executive Officer and Assistant Operations Officer and they probably wanted to make an example of us to everyone else. I told myself, if we are put on copilot status I didn't want to stay overseas so it looked like I'd be home soon, that is, if they didn't recommend that we serve additional time overseas.

Finally we moved to a new area, the old Japanese headquarters for veterinarians. It was really something to see. There was one building that was completely filled with horseshoes stacked in neat rows. I'd never seen so many horseshoes in my life. At that time Colonel Roth cut orders putting Kennedy and me on copilot status for the rest of the time we were overseas. We never had a chance to present our side of the story and we felt that we didn't deserve this punishment. That was the last straw. We said the hell with it and gave up any idea of staying overseas for promotion. I decided to get home as soon as I could. Kennedy was able to go home the next day because he had 79 points. I would not be able to leave for some time because I only had 72 points. I needed 75 more hours to be eligible to come home on rotation and my 14 months was going to be up on November 20. I thought I had one more chance of going home on points if I got my Air Medal, which would give me five more points for a total of 77. There was nothing to do but wait and see.

As it turned out, there still was a shortage of 1st Pilots, so a few weeks later I was promoted back to 1st Pilot status.[51]

Early on September 29th they woke me up and wanted me to fly with Colonel Ames, who was the commanding officer of the 375th group, *The Tokyo Trolley*. He was on his way home and needed to fly to Nichols field in Manila. When we took off he wanted to see some of Japan before he went home, so we flew over Tokyo and he took pictures. He was pilot and I was his co-pilot. Next we climbed up to 13,000 feet and circled around Mt. Fuji, then flew over Hiroshima and I'm telling you, there was nothing left. I've never seen anything like it. From there we flew to Nagasaki where they dropped the second bomb. It was even worse. The bomb just obliterated the town. We flew on to Kanoya in southern Japan and then to Okinawa, flying 1500 miles in a day of just sightseeing. It was really interesting. The Colonel took his Jeep with him in the plane so when we landed somewhere, like in Okinawa, Colonel Ames would call the ground crew and have them unload his Jeep so he could drive around and go to his meetings or sightseeing. The Colonel stayed in Okinawa a couple days to take care of some business, and then we flew to Manila to see about his transportation home. He told me, if he had a couple extra days, we would go to Hong Kong and Shanghai, but that didn't work out. It was nice to fly with Colonel Ames and be able to go wherever you wanted to just see the country.[52]

I finally dropped Colonel Ames off at Nichols field in Manila and then I flew back to Clark Field. On the trip back I had the Colonel's Jeep on the plane to use as I pleased. I stayed at Clark Field a couple of days and drove north to Tarlac to visit my WAC girlfriend. In Tarlac there was an Army station with a number of women employed as code breakers. Next I flew to Okinawa on my way back to Tokyo. When I landed, I would call up the tower and announce that this was the Colonel's aircraft and would they please send out the ground crew to "Unload the Colonel's Jeep," They didn't seem to notice, or maybe didn't care, that the Colonel was not on the plane on the return trip. I had to stay on Okinawa a couple of days because of a typhoon in the Tokyo area, and it was nice to have the Jeep to run around in. When I returned to Tokyo I was surprised to find that everybody who had 75 points or over had left the outfit and gone to a replacement Battalion to go home.

Meanwhile I was living on the base in a room with eleven guys. The rooms were clean and a welcome change from jungle living. Each area had a pot-bellied stove for heating. I was always cold so I moved my cot close to the stove to keep me warm during my deep sleep. We all got along pretty well and we had an apartment, or what was really a hotel room in the Marunouchi hotel in Tokyo. We shared the cost and kept it so that anybody in the gang could go to Tokyo on the weekend.

The idea of being a copilot was quite a blow to my morale at the time. I was one of the oldest guys in the squad then and the idea of being just a copilot made it worse. That little episode did not go on my record but the outcome made me sad. Around the same time one of our airplanes cracked up down at Kanoya field on the island of Kyushu. The pilot was one of the new ones I had checked out. He undershot the field and hit a tree on the approach. The airplane burned but nobody was hurt, including the 20 nurses he had on board.

The days passed and I still had no word about whether or not I could go home. That was on the mind of all of us, and soon became a burning preoccupation, especially since we found ourselves just sitting around, with nothing to do. In early November a couple of my buddies and I discovered a new pastime, a way to make the time pass. We found a private country club and golf course—the Koganei Country Club—not far from Tachikawa. We'd go into the locker room, open up a locker, and use a set of golf clubs we'd find there. I always brought some candy bars because there were little Japanese kids hanging around the golf course. When I'd hit a ball into the rough, I'd give a kid a candy bar if he could find it. They were smart kids. One time I had just about given up looking and saw a kid standing there. By then they knew us. The kid held out his hand and I gave him a candy bar. He lifted his foot, reached down and handed me my ball, and then ran off to enjoy his reward. With nothing else to do, we started going there and playing golf every day. It kept us from thinking about how bad we wanted to go home.

Incidentally, today the Koganei Country Club has the most exclusive golf course in the world. Memberships are reported to cost US$2 million to US$3 million. Meanwhile, while we were golfing, it was getting closer to Christmas but I was not getting any closer to going home. Something would break in a couple weeks, I kept telling myself.

One afternoon the first 31st Calvary put on a rodeo in Tokyo. On the radio I heard that there were 55,000 GIs in the stadium to watch the rodeo. Three P-38s were going to do a flyby accompanied by a double Immelman in formation over the stadium. Another pilot, Dusty Rhodes and I decided to go to the strip and take a plane over the stadium where we could get a bird's eye view of the rodeo. That was one compensation we had, the ability to take a plane whenever we wanted to fly over Tokyo. It made me think that someday I hoped I could to fly over the Coliseum in Los Angeles!

In mid-November Charlie Reid, the squad adjutant, sent my orders in to go home, but the Wing told him to hold up for a while. They didn't give any reason. Meanwhile I was selected to lead a formation that was practicing for an air show. The Fifth Air Force was going to put on an air show up at Sendai about 250 miles north of Tokyo. It was frustrating when all around me it seemed that everybody was going home. Things were really winding down. Almost all the strips at Okinawa were closed except Yontan, and in the Philippines all the strips were closed except Clark, Nichols, and Nielson which were on Luzon and several others in the southern Philippines. To top it off, I still had not been paid for 3 1/2 months, was broke, and owed money to my buddies. In compensation, I was playing golf almost every day. And, we finally had all the beer we could drink. A new rotation plan of seven months and 450 hours went into effect but the catch was you had to have a replacement. I would be the first one in our squad to go home if we got someone to replace me. We needed three more pilots. I was hopeful that my orders would go in and if everything went smoothly I'd be home for Christmas. It was a nice to dream anyway, but of course it didn't happen.

A few days before Thanksgiving, I finally got a mission. I was ordered to go to Nielson Field near Manila, a flight of 2,000 miles. There I had to pick up a load of 25 nurses, who had just come over from the States at the 22nd replacement center. There was snow all over the ground in the morning when we took off. Our first stop was Okinawa and fortunately the weather was beautiful—SAVANNA ONE. From Okinawa on down to Nielson, the weather continued to be good.

Two days later, loaded up and on the field at Nielson, the weather turned bad and I decided to wait until it cleared up. No sense taking any chances this late in the game. Instead, we went into Manila to spend the evening. Manila had changed dramatically—it was all cleaned up. All of rubble and trash had been cleared away and it did not look like the war-torn Manila I remembered. The next morning we were still grounded because of weather, so we went back into Manila. It was the day before Thanksgiving, so we planned to either have dinner in Manila, or if the weather cleared we could spend Thanksgiving at Laoag at the northern tip of Luzon, which is what we did.

On November 22, Thanksgiving, the weather was SAVANNA FIVE when we took off for Okinawa. As we passed Lingayen Gulf we learned that the weather was deteriorating. I decided to continue for a while and if it was bad, turn around and return to Laoag. We went on for four hours and were about two hours out of Okinawa when we met a cold front that was moving in on Okinawa. The weather report was now SAVANNA FOUR, so I turned around and headed back towards Laoag.

Army DUKW, aka Duck

At this point my worry was the fuel situation. Normally we should be able to stay up about nine hours, so our gas would last until we got back, plus an hour's reserve, if we had no problems.

As it was, we made it back okay, with 400 gallons of gas left. At Laoag we all had dates and went into town in an Army DUKW, affectionately known as a "Duck." The Duck is an amphibious vehicle—a boat with six wheels.[53] We used the Duck because a road between the strip and town was cut off by a river where the bridges were bombed out. We went to a nightclub called the Tower with a bunch of nurses and enjoyed ourselves. The next morning we tried again and this time made it to Okinawa where we spent the evening over at the nurses' quarters playing bridge. The following day we took them to Kure, near Hiroshima. All in all we had a good time on that trip. It was better than sitting around and got my mind off waiting for my orders to go home. At the time, everybody at the base was receiving Christmas packages. I no longer thought that I'd make it back by Christmas.

Back in the waiting game, it was raining and very cold. Several other fellows, (Ed Roberts and Sid Shuchster), and I decided that we were going to get on a train and take a trip around the islands. We were getting impatient sitting around. We decided go south and then come back north on the train. One of our pilots flew us down to Hiroshima where we stayed with the 10th Corps at Kure, the big Japanese naval base. Hiroshima looked worse on the ground than it did from the air. It was completely demolished. When we drove through the town it was quiet and peaceful. Everything was dead, no plants, just debris everywhere and very little activity. Very few Japanese were walking the streets. The road between Hiroshima and Kure is along the waterfront.

Hiroshima after the Bomb

Much of the Japanese war material was lying along the roadside such as bombs, aircraft engines, and torpedoes. As we approached Kure, naval equipment was plentiful. At Kure we were housed in Japanese naval cadet quarters. The rooms were cold but clean. There were two Japanese aircraft carriers in the harbor and some small ships, besides the ships from our Navy. From Kure we planned to go by train to Kobe, Kyoto, Osaka, and Nagoya, and then back to Tokyo.

The nurses we'd brought up from Manila had moved to a little island about 10 miles out in the bay from Hiroshima called Eta Jima and we decided that we'd go visit them before continuing on our trip. The nurses found us a place to stay in an empty hospital ward. Our girls were not working the first day we got there, so we played tennis and looked over the Naval Academy.[54] It is really a beautiful place, nicely landscaped with trees and shrubbery. At night we would go to the club and dance. For three days we played basketball, tennis and danced at night. The Navy was going to blow up some explosives at the other end of the island so we had to move away temporarily. We decided to go on a hike and have a picnic. In the middle of the picnic we had some excitement when the explosion rocked the whole island. All in all it was a wonderful time with the nurses. From Eta Jima, we returned to Honshu, where we rode the train all day through many cities, finally getting back to Tokyo about midnight.

Christmas was coming closer, so several of us picked out a Christmas tree in case we were still In Japan for the holiday. There was every indication that we'd still be there. We were flying more missions, most of the time carrying personnel, but we've had a few cargo loads also. One plane went to Okinawa to pick up 8000 pounds of paper cups. We had a lot of strange cargos. Whenever we moved our base to a new location, we basically had to tear everything down and take it with us. So if we had a control tower at one airfield, when we moved it would be taken apart, the pieces loaded on one of our planes, we would haul it to the new location where the control tower would be reassembled. A plane was going to Korea to bring back a load of silkworms. The idea was to re-start the silk industry. We were supposed to disinfect the airplane every time we went to Okinawa, the Philippines or any malarial area. We kidded the pilot about spraying the ship with aerosol when we brought silkworms back. I got to visit Seoul, riding as copilot with the operations officer. This was during my "suspension," November 3-5. We spent a few days and looked around the city before coming back. I stayed with some guys from the 317th Troop Carrier group. This flight was tricky, because we couldn't fly above 2,000 feet or the silk worms would die. We had to figure out a route through passes around the mountains that kept us below this elevation. We also brought back a load of Hawaiians who were going home.[55]

With Christmas a scant two weeks away, I was officer of the day for the group and when I reported for duty, the adjutant said "Mosier let's see, yes, you now have five more points, your Air Medal came through." That gave me 77 points and officers' points had gone down to 73, but the rules stipulated that you could only go home under one system. I had already applied for orders to go home on rotation, so I had to wait until those orders came back. At this point, I wrote home and told my mother,

"Don't write me anymore, because I'll be on my way home within the next 10 days and probably in the States around New Year's. When I say don't write, I mean it because this is the real thing now. I should be leaving the squadron in another five days. It's going to be swell to see home again. I've looked forward to this for so long it will probably be a letdown. Keep the Christmas tree up until I get home. Your loving son, Bob"

Christmas came and went and I was still waiting on orders. For Christmas, my present was to get all my inoculations up-dated. I got one for influenza, one for cholera and one for plague. Then a few days later I got tetanus and another plague shot, and also had some dental work done.

Christmas 1945 was my third Christmas away from home and my second overseas. I don't know why, but this Christmas was about the saddest one I'd ever had. I'd never been as homesick as I was during those last few days. Every time I heard Christmas Carols it made me think of home and all the good things connected with it. I could picture my Mom, sister, and my brother Jack and his new wife Laurie—the whole family—almost as if I was there. Christmas eve I went to midnight mass with some of the gang. It was a beautiful service and I prayed for everyone at home. This was one of the most grateful Christmases we'd had in several years. We should all be thankful that the war was over and that our family was still together and well. It was very seldom that I got sentimental when I wrote home, but that night I listened to Bing Crosby singing *Silent Night* and it made me think of home and of the family. I could picture the front room with a Christmas tree and all the trimmings and everybody sitting around just glowing with happiness.

At last, 1945 ended. As the New Year began, I was still waiting on orders. I was through flying. I had my flying time in for the month. I really had a great time on New Year's Eve. We first went to a USO show and into the Wing club. We really took the club over. The party did not break up until about three in the morning. Some more days passed. Finally in January my orders came through and I boarded an aircraft carrier for the trip back home, with destination Seattle.

My war with Japan had finally ended.

The Air Medal is given to "those who distinguish themselves by meritorious achievment while participating in aerial flight and must be accomplished with distinction above that normally expected... to recognize single actions of merit or sustained operational activities against the enemy." [40]

PART V

HOME AJUSTMENT • MEET BEVERLY • UNIVERSITY • FAMILY • CAREER COLLINS RADIO COMPANY • TECHNOLOGY INNOVATION • ADVANCING COMMUNICATION • WWWEB • COMMUNITY SERVICE.

Bob and Collins Radio Apollo Team

CHAPTER 20

HOMEWARD BOUND

Bob: I was finally shipped back to the U.S. on a small aircraft carrier (an escort carrier), 21 days, no stops, destination Seattle. On the carrier, we put a high fence around the flight deck so we could play baseball. Any ball hit over the fence was an automatic "out." Food on the ship was plentiful and for the first time we had some improvements over what we'd had in Japan. Every day during the voyage we could buy sundries, chocolate candy and other goodies at the onboard PX.

When we pulled in to Seattle, I was momentarily shocked when I saw Mt. Rainer—it looked like Mt. Fuji, and for a moment I thought we were back in Japan! As soon as I could get leave and arrange for transportation, I had one thought in mind. I wanted to get back to Los Angeles, see my mother, wear civilian clothes, eat my favorite foods, and look up my old friends.

As we arrived at the Navy dock in Seattle everyone was on the flight deck watching the docking. There were so many returning soldiers on deck that the heavy load of people standing on the starboard side made the flight deck lean down towards the dock at about a 20 degree list. The captain and sailors were having a hard time securing their lines. As the ship slowly slid in towards the dock all of us were looking at the girls standing on the dock with the Marine color guard flags and marching band standing in the background. Most of the women were greeting their returning sailor boyfriends or their long-absent husbands. It was a wonderful sight and I had a deep sense of relief and success to really be home safe and sound. Even the wounded troops that were staging on the decks below, could now forget their injuries for a few moments. One of the first things I can recall, as I got off the ship, was the taste of fresh milk. We were handed milk after we disembarked. Having it for the first time in many months was wonderful. It tasted so much better than the powdered milk we drank overseas.

We were marched off to the Seattle train station in town for the trip home to Southern California. The train ride took a couple of days, but as we watched the scenery pass by we could not control our emotions of extreme happiness after winning the war with Japan and making it home safely. The scenery on the trip south was beautiful. The vegetation along the route was green and lush and well-groomed. At every station local people lined the sidelines waving flags and welcoming us home with words like "job well done."

When I arrived in Los Angeles I was processed at the separation center located at Fort MacArthur. California. My date of relief from active duty was March 7, 1946.

I was interrogated by a nice looking but very professional Army WAC. She was filling out a form called "Military Record and Report of Separation, Certificate Of Service." It listed my military history including my specialty as a "Pilot Twin Engine 1051' and that I participated in the Pacific War in the following campaigns: Bismark Archipelago, Luzon, Northern Solomons, Southern Philippines, Western Pacific and New Guinea. It listed decorations and campaigns as Air Medal, Philippine Liberation Ribbon, World War II Victory Medal, American Theater Service Medal, and the Asiatic Pacific Theater Service Medal. It was an incomplete record of my total service, but I didn't care about making it perfect. I just felt good about participating and doing my duty. I left the center feeling free and ready to have some fun being a civilian.

I looked forward to a reunion with my brother Jack, and meeting his wife Laurie, my new sister-in-law. Jack got his commission as a 2nd lieutenant in May, 1945, a year after me, and trained as a bombardier. He became an instructor at airfields in Texas and Arkansas and did not have to go overseas. My sister Mary promised to introduce me to a bunch of her girlfriends when I came home. That was something I really looked forward to!

Beverly: During the war years we very young girls had worked our way into an adult life style since war created a need for women in the work force. Neither I nor my friends were true adults yet.

Thus those of us tall enough passed as being grown up every day in many ways, but everyone I knew was far under the age of 18 in a time when 21 was considered adult. I was twelve and tall. We young workers were responsible and considered ourselves good at our various jobs, while at the same time we were quite naive about many other things.

Sex, for example. We were taught that "nice girls" waited for marriage for that and with the lack of desirable boys, as nearly all of the interesting guys were off fighting the war—we naturally wondered, what would come of us? Meanwhile, we worked our little tails off doing what the men were not around to do: simple, low paying, but interesting and fun jobs.

We grew up just dreaming of that prince who would come home one day and change all of that.

Then they did. They came home. But guess what? By the hundreds and thousands they came home bringing what was known as a "War Bride," a young woman they had met and fallen for in whichever country they found themselves when the fighting stopped. Even former enemies became wives!

Magazines and newspapers heralded those war-bride arrivals as the ships arrived from all the oceans. But what about us? We had been waiting for our young men to return and marry us!

My friends and I felt abandoned as we talked about it and wondered. Then one of the girls brought to our attention an article that actually remembered that we were here on the home front. This article made a suggestion, a stupid suggestion as it turned out—as the author tried to solve the problem.

It read: "With so many of our young men killed at war and the ones returning home already married, our young women will have no, or little, chance of marrying and having children." We hadn't even thought of that yet! Then it was suggested that perhaps the men should be allowed to, under these new circumstances, take a second wife.

We girls read it with disgust. We were all appalled and agreed on one thing: "No way!" Not one of us was willing to share a man. If we didn't marry, we didn't. That was just too bad for us. We would find something else to do with our lives. We had missed Proms and things at school without men. We had interesting jobs while they were gone and we could continue to carry on, if we had to, without a man. Not what we had desired, but we would be all right. We wouldn't like it, but there seemed no option. It was sad, but we shook it off and laughed about it and parted with the decision that it was a man of our own, or no man!

The men came home, for the most part eager to take up where they left off, surprised in many cases to find that they had survived to start life anew and were now trying to find a job or go to college. We girls forgot the scare of that man-less life predicted for us, and were happy to find quite a few much more grown up men returning, no longer the boys who had left school. They had changed into experienced men with lots of ideas about what they wanted now. Happily, we seemed to be one of those things they wanted. I expected to be one of those wives. It never occurred to any of us that we were too young back then. We had all been working since age twelve and felt experienced and ready for whatever life brought. Now it was just a matter of meeting up with the right guy.

CHAPTER 21

LIFE RESUMED

Bob: After I was discharged in February of 1946, I was gladly, willingly and happily relieved to be out of the military; separated from the armed forces—airplanes and all—that I had worked so hard to join. For those first months I didn't even miss flying. It hadn't occurred to me that I would not find time to pilot an airplane again—ever. In fact, even though I had not done anything about it as yet, the news that Arizona had a huge desert parking lot covered with the government's surplus planes of all kinds and conditions that could be purchased for a dime on the dollar was of great interest to me. I knew I would go out there soon and see if a plane was waiting for me to just come and claim it. The airplane money in my account waited.

I arrived home back in the States ready to begin that relaxation I had been looking forward to. In fact I had written my mother telling her she should use some of the money I sent her to buy a big, comfortable, easy chair. I think I hinted that I planned to sit in it and never get up. That sounded so good after all the nights spent sleeping under the wing of my airplane at the mercy of the beach crabs that wandered out at night and the green mold that formed overnight on my shoes so I had to clean them inside and out before I could put them on again—after I shook out the creepy things that had crawled in.

Finally home at last I looked at the large, over-stuffed chair Mom had bought. Mom was proud to show me the letter she had obeyed in buying it. I had to laugh as I sat in it for the first time. Mom was disappointed that I scarcely ever sat in it again. I had things to do, friends to get in touch with and new ones to get to know.

My old "Crystal Beach" gang of school buddies began to gather each night in Les's Bar, a small neighborhood joint in Hollywood nearby the Malt Shop where we had met so often in the past, as we waited to join the war, each in a different way. Everyone was happy to see us returning one by one, just as we had left.

By some very good luck we all made it safely home from the Army, Navy, Marines and the Merchant Marines. My best friend, Fred "Cliff" Clifford, had chosen the Merchant Marine for a couple of reasons. The pay was very good, not token like the services, they did not own you body and brain as the services did, and you came and went as you pleased. It was still dangerous. The enemy submarines would blast them to the bottom the same as any other ship.

The drawback was that because you had received top wages and did not belong to a service, you were not eligible for the benefits of the G.I. Bill. As a Merchant Marine, you worked for a private Company.

So it was almost a miracle that we all made it home, with the exception of Kazie's younger brother who had died in the war. His name is inscribed permanently on a wall of John Marshall High School, along with some others we did not know, who remain remembered as Marshall's heroes lost to the War.

We moved the party each night to a different home to greet the familiar parents and retell our tales. This prolonged reunion took up most of my time. My sister Mary had a new boyfriend, Richard Woodrum, who had a nice car that he occasionally lent to me. She also had some girl friends at the Telephone Company where she worked that she was anxious for me to meet. I was willing and looking forward to meeting them too, but for now gathering in more and more of the old friends and talking about what we did or what we wanted to do next was most time consuming. A transit strike changed all that and sealed my fate.

Beverly: I knew Bob was a pilot. Also, I had been led to believe, by people who claimed to know the facts, that the best and smartest young men were the ones selected for that coveted job as pilots. Thus, I was impressed by Bob even before I actually met him in person. I definitely wanted an intelligent man. Smart was number one on my list followed by all of the regular stuff like, sense of humor, good manners, fine friends and sort of good to look at. Luckily money hadn't made the list. Bob didn't have any more than I did, which was not much. When we met, in person, he was so handsome and personable that I was blown away. He was exactly the kind of fellow I had dreamed about finding to be my husband someday. But someday was so far away, as it always is, that I hadn't really been giving his discovery much thought.

A few days after Bob returned home there was a transportation strike and no public transportation was operating. Mary and I were stranded at the telephone company. Mary said that she would call her brother and have him come pick me up and take me home. I told her no, I would call my Dad. That day at noon, Bob called the office. He said, "I'm coming by to take you home."

I said, "No, my father is coming to pick me up." Bob replied, "Well, call him and tell him not to come, because otherwise he'll have to drive home alone."

At this I finally agreed to let Bob take me home.

After that we went out every night. I was immediately attracted to his easy-going personality, his sense of humor. I was only eighteen and had not dated much, but I admired the fact that he had gone to war right out of high school and served his country by flying all over dangerous South Pacific islands delivering men and equipment and transporting the wounded to hospitals. One night we drove up and parked on Mulholland Drive with another couple, his friend Russ Kibbe and another girl. You could see the entire Los Angeles/Hollywood area lit up below. It was a clear, starry night. Bob said, "Let's take a walk." We got out of the car and walked for a while, dazzled by the city lights below all sparkling in the darkness, and then talked for a while. Every now and then Bob would glance back at the car. Finally he said, "Okay, we can go back now."

As we drove back down the hill I heard Russ's girlfriend lean over and say to him "After we take Bev home, I want you to bring Bob back up here and leave him with me while you take a walk, Okay?"

We got to my house and Bob got out of the car and walked me up to my front door. I was so mad I couldn't see straight. I didn't say a word, I just turned around and punched him as hard as I could in the side of the face. Then I ran in the house.

About fifteen minutes later the phone rang and it was Bob.

"What was that all about?" he said.

I said, "Where are you?" "At home," he replied, "why?"

"So you didn't go back up on Mulholland with that girl?" I said.

"No, of course not," he replied. "She's not my type." I believed him; I knew that he hadn't had enough time to go back up the hill and then go home and call me.

We continued to go out, dancing, or sometimes to one of his friend's where the guys would sit around and trade war stories. For those of us who had been at the home front, the stories were always interesting, in some cases, almost unbelievable, to hear what our young men had done. The war stories stopped one day when the veterans got together and decided it was time to forget the war.

As the days and weeks passed, we grew closer together. There was some vital connection that seemed to grow between us.

Three months after we met we were married. I was eighteen years old.

Bob: The day I picked Beverly up at the Telephone Company office, we stopped by the local Drive-In on the way to her house and I introduced her to some of my Crystal Beach friends. I wanted all my buddies to see what an attractive date I had. Beverly seemed to comfortably fit in and she was enthusiastically accepted on that first night as one of the Crystal Beach Gang, as we called ourselves. After that first time, I borrowed a different car each night, taking Beverly with me to meetings with my old gang, where she enjoyed getting to know them and listen to their war stories. Within two weeks of our nightly dates I had decided that she was the wife I wanted.

I had been bringing Beverly home from our dates and then spending the night, what was left of it, on her parent's living room couch, to be there to take her back to work in the morning, because the transportation strike was still going on. Every evening I borrowed whatever car was available to me, to take her out in the evening and back to work in the morning at five A.M.

I was still interested in flying and found out that the Army Air Force was staging war surplus aircraft in Wickenburg Arizona for sale to the public. Several of my buddies suggested we go together to Arizona to look at the aircraft for sale. Beverly was at work and the strike had ended, so we planned the trip in one of the available cars. We all enjoyed the trip to Arizona and had fun looking over the miles of airplanes, parked in the desert where the hot, dry, air helped to preserve them.

Many others were wandering about looking for a plane to own or to find a part from one being scraped to improve the craft they now owned, or just looking and wondering what battles each had seen. All of my buddies had a different plane they wanted me to buy. I was called to come and look at this one and then that one.

Someone suggested, "Get one big enough to carry us all!"

"Oh and who will foot the bill for the fuel to fly that big thing?" I asked. Even though I had a soft spot for my big, old, twin engine advanced trainer, the AT-17 "Bamboo Bomber," I knew I couldn't afford it.

As I carefully looked over the candidates of my choice, it was difficult to choose between the modern small planes and the old one I had soloed in, one that had two wings and some character. Slowly, I began to know what I would do. I picked out several aircraft that I was interested in buying. However, I returned home without buying one. I decided to wait until I could find a local airport and hanger space for either a single engine Primary Trainer PT-17 or a single engine Basic Trainer BT-13, both available at bargain prices. The twin engine Advance Trainer AT-17 was beyond my financial capability.

Back at home thoughts of airplanes were temporarily forgotten. I told my sister Mary that I was going to ask Beverly to marry me. I was smitten with her the first time I met her. I wanted to take her in my arms forever.

Mary said, "Oh don't buy a ring until I show you the one she wants. We used to look in the windows and show each other the ring sets we liked. I know exactly where it is on Hollywood Boulevard, not far from work."

It was August 23rd and Beverly's Dad's birthday. I went to her house on Oakshire Drive and showed Beverly's Dad the ring set I'd bought and asked for his approval to marry his beautiful daughter—the oldest of his three girls. The entire Christiansen family was sitting in their living room watching and listening to what I was saying. I was very anxious, standing there in my Army uniform, not knowing what he would say. Receiving his approval, I held the open ring box out for Beverly. She smiled and said "Yes" with a hug and kiss. We all were very happy, Beverly's mother, Billie, her Dad, Chris, and her two sisters, Avalon and Carol. From then on I was part of the Christiansen family.

As she excitedly accepted my proposal and ring, she realized how I had learned of her choice, as there was only one way—Mary. The velvet box contained a ¼ carat diamond in the engagement ring banded by twin bands of white gold against the yellow gold, with a wedding band that matched it and the wedding band I would wear, a larger duplicate. Better yet, the one she had chosen, I could actually afford—if I didn't buy an airplane. I had looked the war surplus planes over and liked them. But between a plane and Beverly, I immediately knew which I would choose—Beverly as my wife. Beverly wore that ring for twenty five years until it simply wore out. I replaced it with a ring with a much larger emerald cut stone and she wore that one twenty five years also. On our golden wedding anniversary, I told her she could choose a new set of rings if she wanted to.

Many years later, during a family gathering that included our 4 children and their spouses with their 14 nearly grown children, one of the grandsons asked about my failure to buy that grand old airplane when I had the chance.

"It was either an airplane or your grandmother!" I told them all. Some of them laughed and they all agreed as one shouted out: "We think that was the best choice you ever made!" It was a compliment, not just of Grandma Bev, but also in appreciation of their own existence!

As I lost that first chance, and as it turned out, my last chance to have my own plane, I knew it would require more money and care than I would have time to give to it if I entered college and spent the next four years becoming an electrical engineer. That was also when I changed our original plan to be engaged for about two years. I knew UCLA would require my full attention. I could not be running back and forth from the Westwood campus to Hollywood every night to see Beverly and still make my grades. Instead, we got married in two weeks and we both headed off for my schooling together and, what the heck, started a family right away! It seemed to me that we would be in no position to travel or

Little Church of Hollywood Wedding

do anything but school for the next four years. Then, when I graduated and found a job, the kids would be old enough to take with us, when we had money to do anything. Bev agreed and that was how we started our family.

Beverly: After we were married Bob started classes and I went back to work. Not longer after that I thought I was coming down with something I must have caught on our honeymoon. Boy did I call that right! I just didn't know what yet. I often had to get quick relief from the Telephone Switch Board; I was stuck there for two hours at a time. As soon as my supervisor took my place, I'd dash to the break room and the toilet to throw up. In between I felt just fine, but after two days of that I went to see a doctor.

He said, "I suspect that you are pregnant, but we'll know for sure when you miss your next period. Come back in two weeks." All of those simple but accurate pregnancy tests that one takes for granted in this century had not been invented yet.

Like so many others at that time after the war, we started our married life with virtually no money, but somehow things always seemed to work out. The story of how our first daughter Nancy came into the world is an example. On many occasions I had walked past the Hollywood Hospital and noticed the many pregnant ladies going into a building, actually a little old wooden house, right next door to the hospital. The name above the door read; "Hollywood Presbyterian Barite Maternity Clinic." I decided to go in and inquire. If I was expecting, I would need a doctor, so perhaps this Hollywood Hospital Clinic was a possibility.

There was a lady behind a desk just inside the door. So I asked, "Is this the part of the hospital that takes care of maternity cases?"

"Not all, but some. Are you expecting?"

I told her I wasn't sure, but would know in a couple of weeks. I was trying to find out where I should go then and, more importantly, how much it would cost. I knew that sounded a little late in my planning, but better late than never, right?

She laughed and then answered that the cost was based on the husband's salary. "How much does your husband make a month?"

I answered. "He's going to go to school on the G.I. Bill and they pay his school costs and will start to send us a check for $90.00 each month to live on, as soon as the paper work is processed." I started to tell her what I made a month, but she interrupted me.

"We don't count your income, as it won't last." Little did I know, but she got that right! After a little bit of writing and figuring, she gave me the answer. "Your cost will be $60.00"

Wow! I was expecting her to say something in the hundreds. Or did she mean each month? Oh and I forgot the hospital. "Do you know what the hospital will charge?" I asked.

"We are associated with this hospital. What we charge covers everything." She smiled. "Even if you need to have a Caesarean, it's all the same. For your case, a total of $60." My expression told her that I was thrilled. "I think my husband will be very happy about this," I said. "So how does it work?"

"You will be given a schedule for regular visits, and then when the baby is ready, you will be admitted to the hospital for the birth and three days' rest." This time she did laugh, "and you had better take advantage of it, because when you get home you will not get three days off for a very long time."

At the time, we were living in Bob's mother's home in the Hollywood hills. We were upstairs and Bob's brother and wife Laurie lived downstairs. With the baby on the way, Bob fixed up the basement of a home in Glendale owned by one of his uncles, and we moved there.

When my supervisor learned that I was pregnant, she was very nice as she told me that I might as well quit work now, before I threw up all over my switch board and put a whole circuit out of order for hours. In other words I was politely fired.

Our first child, a baby girl, was born on Monday, July 27, 1947. "Seven pounds and two ounces," The nurse announced and "Oh look!" she said, "Just look at that gorgeous red hair!" We named her Nancy Carol.

Surprise! We were not alone in our plan for a family. UCLA put in rows of old Army barracks on Gayley Avenue in Westwood, California, just past the UCLA football field. The two story wooden buildings held only veterans with wives and children while we all were getting our degrees of one kind or another. The development was nick-named Gayley Ville.

Bob: We revisited the area when our two oldest daughters registered at UCLA twenty years later. Gayley Ave had lost the barracks and now sported several, tall, first class dormitories to house students. The football field I used to cross to get to class was the same.

In Gayley Ville days our whole group worked together like an over-sized family to help one another, as we were all just squeaking by money-wise. The G.I. Bill paid my UCLA expenses plus $90.00 a month for living expenses. I was working part time as an electrician for the H. B. Chapman Company in Los Angeles. Going to school and working to support the family, I did not have much time for social activities. I lost contact with all my friends until after I graduated. Anytime anyone in Galey Ville received a bonus gift of produce from someone's garden or fruit tree, they shared it around. We did the same with rabbit meat, fresh fruit and bee honey that we received from Beverly's Dad as gifts from his home in the Hollywood hills.

The family downstairs from us in Gayley Ville had the only phone on the block. This neighbor managed a babysitting service for folks outside of Gayley Ville. People with local homes could call her and she would either take the job herself or find someone who would take it. It was easy because we all needed the money and we were home studying so our wives could leave for the evening. We became good fathers taking care of the little ones while doing homework when our wives were babysitting late into the night for 50 cents an hour. Somehow we got by, although it seemed we were always running out of money only a day or two before the next check.

After three years UCLA let me know that I would have to go to Berkeley to finish my degree in electronic engineering. UCLA was just getting started in Westwood, and only offered a General Engineering degree, while I wanted an EE degree. The work for my final year could only be completed in Berkeley's new up-to-date labs. Thus we were not eligible to live in the UCLA housing over the summer as I was not registered to be at UCLA the following semester.

I drove up to Berkeley alone to register for university housing. They told me that I had to bring the whole family there before they could assign me living facilities. They had a much larger complex of two story silver buildings. They were built along the edge of the water in Albany to house mostly shipyard workers during the war.

When I was informed that I could not be given an apartment until the whole family was there in the office, I admitted that we could not do that just yet. I said, "We're waiting for the new baby—our second. We'll be here the week before school starts. See you then, but before I go, can you tell me one thing—why are all the buildings painted silver?"

She smiled, admitting they were a bit odd, but told me, "The job of painting them was given to the Navy and that color was what they had plenty of to spare." I guess that made sense. But the surprise of the interior painting of our apartment still awaited us.

We had a two year old, Nancy, and our second child was due in August. Bev wanted to stay near to her doctor and the same hospital where she had given birth to Nancy. The closest place was right up the hill from the Hollywood Hospital, my mother's house. My sister Mary had married Richard and moved out. Jack had built a room on downstairs where he and Laurie lived with their baby Andalee. We moved in and lived upstairs with my mother. Then I got a full time job as an electrician, again working for the H. B. Chapman Company, to save as much money as possible for that last year of school.

On August 14th 1949 our second daughter Pamela Ann was born and four weeks later we piled what we could carry onto our 1937 Ford sedan I'd bought for $25. It was an old car but seemed to run okay and it had made the first trip north to Berkeley without a problem.

This trip north was almost trouble free. The car quit once and I got out to look under the hood, where I determined that it was starving of fuel. The fuel pump was in need of repair. We were on a lonely road with no help in sight, so I rummaged in the glove compartment hoping to find something with which to fix it. I found a stick of chewing gum and a band aid and figured that ought to do it.

Actually it was a simple temporary fix that I hoped would get the four of us the rest of the way. I assumed that the fuel pump diaphragm was not pumping. It was using a push rod riding on a motor cam to work the pump diaphragm. I needed a new pump, however I was going to make a makeshift repair by stuffing the band aid with gum into the pump housing making the push rod have a longer stroke in the hopes that it would pump gas long enough to make it to a repair garage. Making strange things do in a pinch was common in the Pacific War. The temporary fix worked fantastically all the way to Berkeley and much later I sold the Ford as is, still fixed with the band aid and gum. For years Bev loved to tell the story of how her engineer husband repaired a car with chewing gum and a band aid.

It was freezing cold in Albany. A chilling wind blew across the San Francisco Bay. With two babies in the car the housing office was quick to give us the keys to an apartment that was recently vacated. I hoped we could get it warm. I had been born across the Bay in San Francisco in the St. Frances hospital facing the Pacific Ocean. There were no memories of it as I was taken to southern California at a very early age. But my mother always said it was cold there and she liked Los Angeles better.

We quickly located our building. The apartments all looked alike, connected by a couple of grass lawns growing from one to the other for blocks and blocks. I was told that my turn to mow the grass would come once a month. Then the key lady added that we were allowed to repaint anything we didn't like or just wanted to at our own expense. Was that statement a pre-warning about something?

We parked and entered the apartment, me carrying Nancy and Beverly holding the baby. I flicked the switch. The electricity was on and the bare light bulb lit up the kitchen side of the big room. Wow! We just stood there staring. The entire room, all of the kitchen walls and cupboards and across to the living room space, the walls, book cases, and even the entire floor were all painted a deep dark blood red! Only the wooden table and four chairs had been spared the red paint. Had they run out of red? There was a brown couch and two arm chairs to match. On the left, the red hallway led to two bedrooms painted red, each having twin beds. For some odd reason the bathroom was white.

We knew without even saying it, that we would be spending our first week, before school started, painting. The floor was cement. Did they just drip so much red paint on it that they just decided to paint it red also? Who knew?

The next day at the Sears store we learned that without a job we could not open a charge account. We didn't have enough cash to buy paint. Nor could we stand the thought of living in that depressing apartment with blood colored everything. The salesman pointed to a table of paint that was on sale. Luckily we had enough money to buy some of the bargain paint. We found two passable colors and bought them, a soft green for the floor and a pale yellow for the walls and cupboards. If only we had enough to cover the red we would be happy.

We opened all of the windows and doors and began to repaint. With babies dressed warm against the cold we painted until we dropped. It was working and the dreary red vanished even under the yellow. We painted ourselves out the door and ate out. On our return we painted the floor into the bed room and went to bed. The green floor looked fine except for one thing. It did not dry overnight. It did not dry over the week end. It actually did not fully dry during the entire year we lived there.

A trip to the Goodwill store found us some cheap raffia rugs that we scattered everyplace. The baby could not ever learn to crawl on a sticky floor, so we bought her a used play pen at the Goodwill store. Nancy learned to do as we did and step from rug to rug whenever possible. If one stepped on the green, there was a "clack" as you lifted your foot from the tacky floor.

School started and I was happy to be studying. It was only for a year, we kept reminding each other. During my last year of studies to get my EE degree, in 1950, I worked as a lab technician part time for Professor Paul Morton to help support my growing family. Dr.

Morton was in the process of designing the first stored Basic program computer controlled calculator for the University. The calculator was using an 8-bit digital control software system entered manually, one 8-bit word at a time, with manually selected on/off switches. We stored the information using twin triode tubes for each binary bit storage. The software program required more memory to store the words entered. The storage method chosen was to use a magnetic drum memory.

I was assigned to help Professor Morton in this design. We obtained an aluminum drum twelve inches in diameter and 18 inches high driven by a motor at 3600 revolutions per minute. We needed to coat the drum with a magnetic material and build magnetic pick up devices to have magnetic tracks around the drum where we could read and write digital words. My first attempt used ¼ inch magnetic tape glued to the drum surface. The first time we started up, as the drum was spinning up to speed the tape flew off in bits and pieces all over the lab. No one was hurt except I was embarrassed by the failure. The next try was to spray multiple coats of a magnetic paint onto the drum. This worked and we finished this calculator design that could add and multiply small numbers with a 6 foot rack of vacuum tubes and a magnetic drum. All this machinery had much less capability than today's $10 hand calculator.

The year passed. When I took my last final I came home to find that Bev had packed everything into one huge box that I found in the trash. Now everything we owned was in it. I took this to mean that Beverly was anxious to leave, so I rented a trailer and had a friend help me put the box up into it and we left to return home to Southern California. School was over for me. I had graduated, but when the class marched for their diplomas I was in Southern California job hunting. About a million of us G.I.s graduated that year and job hunting was difficult. Would we all be able to work at what we had studied to do? It was predictable that as soon as the war ended, many came home, while many high school graduates entered college at the same time.

That first room full of electronics, known as the California Digital Computer (CALDIC), now is a museum piece in the Smithsonian. At graduation, my head was filled with this marvelous, new, unheard of information that I had learned working with Professor Morton on Berkeley's first working computer. "Unheard of" were the key words.

Jobs that would pay me to use this brand new knowledge were not to be found. I took the first work offered as I had a family to support while still searching for that futuristic dream job.

I looked into a job with the Government. I took a series of written tests and passed with an acceptable rating for a GS-5 Engineer. However my first Engineering job was with Douglas Aircraft in Redondo Beach California where I worked on a flush antenna design for a new Navy airplane. I was one of many starting engineers at the time and my table position was so far back in the bull pen that I could not see my boss's office door. So I worked with a head hunter looking for a new opportunity. Then a couple of dream jobs were offered. I was asked to work for the City of Glendale to modernize their electrical power system. It would pay the grand sum of $325 a month and I could do the work, no problem! In fact I could have done that work before I started college! The second job only paid $265 a month, but was the one I chose. It was with Collins Radio Company. The founder, Art Collins, was starting a Western Division of his Company in Burbank California for making remote controlled communications equipment that were unheard of as yet—perfect. Just what I wanted!

Art Collins was a child prodigy when it came to radio. While in high school at age 15, he maintained short wave radio contact with Captain Donald B. MacMillan's 1925 Arctic expedition, using equipment he had designed and built. At the time, the Navy was unable to do this. For 22 days he received Morse code messages from the expedition, wrote them out long hand, rode his bike to the local Western Union telegraph office, and sent them to the National Geographic Society in Washington D.C., where they were released to local newspapers. His abilities brought him to the attention of Admiral Richard E. Byrd. Collins designed and built the radio equipment used by Byrd in his 1933 Antarctica expedition to the South Pole.

Collins R390A Radio

Its successful operation no doubt had a bearing on his later business dealings with the Navy.[56]

I was with Collins for the next 23 years and enjoyed every minute of it—or almost every minute. I was the fifteenth engineer hired for the new Western Division and by the end of my employment I had risen to Assistant Vice President. We had brilliant men and women from all over the world contributing their talents to Art Collin's ideas of digitally remote controlled communications. I felt so lucky to be working with those people that I couldn't believe they were paying me to do it.

After the way we lived for the first four years while I was in college we felt rich with a simple salary. We saved what we could and continued with our well-learned somewhat frugal ways.

Beverly and I had agreed to move our planned next child to a better month. With the girls born in hot months of July and August she wanted to try for an April baby. Our son Robert Rodney Junior was born on Bev's birthday, April 4th, exactly as planned and we were very proud of ourselves for that accomplishment. The girls at ages of three and a half and one and a half smothered the poor little boy with affection and care.

Then, when he was only six weeks old, Bev needed surgery and was ordered to the hospital as soon as possible. Her mother and father took the new baby into their care and Bev's two sisters each added a little girl to their own families and when she came home still unable to care for a small child as she slowly recovered, one child a month came home starting with the oldest as she recovered. Our baby had doubled in age when he was returned. Baby number four (another daughter, as it turned out) would be put off for five years. By then we needed a bigger house, but the problem was that all of our savings were used for the hospital and the surgery.

The same G.I Bill that had sent me to college had a housing bonus for Vets. We could buy a new house, which at the time were being built as fast as possible. To buy one did not require a down payment and the mortgage was at a low interest rate. My brother Jack had just moved into his. We toured their home for the first time. It had cost him $9,000. Mary and Rich paid $10,000. The next tract was showing models so we drove out to Pacoima to see them. This new tract would sell out at $11,500 for a 1,100 sq. ft. home. Why was the price rising so fast? For one thing our house would have built-in appliances. The new architects were finding new inventions to improve houses. We chose a model with a curved driveway in front, leading to a double garage. Asked to choose colors, we chose yellow with white and were on our way to becoming home owners. Then came the catch.

Most of the costs were to be paid by the government. But to keep our name on the model we chose until escrow closed would cost us $50. They called it a non-refundable closing cost. The problem was we didn't have $50. We still drove the old car but until pay day we didn't have fifty cents. There was only one thing we could do to keep the house we had grown so fond of. It was everything we thought we would ever want. We would have to borrow the money somewhere. We were of the generation where borrowing was not usually in our vocabulary, nor were charge accounts. We didn't know many people who could afford to part with that much money, but Mr. Christiansen, Bev's Dad, was happy to lend it to us, especially when he learned that our mortgage had an interest rate of only 4%.He thought that was really a bargain. Our mortgage payment would be lower than our apartment rent. Of course we had to pay taxes and insurance now. I wrote a note saying that I would pay him back at $5 a month for a year. Cash in hand, we drove back to the Valley and handed over the fifty bucks. We spent the next few months visiting our lot to watch impatiently as our beautiful house went up.

CHAPTER 22

AN INVENTIVE CAREER

Bob: When I first went to work for Collins Radio, we were living in a rented Burbank apartment not far from the Collin's Radio Company, so commuting was easy. However things were perking right along and Art Collins often commented that the Burbank office would soon be too small. He said that the Western Division probably should build out in the San Fernando Valley where so much new construction was stretching the City of Los Angeles far beyond its original center. Collins had purchased property there, so we thought that was where the company would eventually relocate. He also was looking for a new location for his corporate headquarters.

Art would disappear for days, traveling back to the corporate headquarters in Cedar Rapids Iowa. The two locations kept him hopping. When he was gone the General Manager, Carl Service, did a good job running things. He was not an engineer so sometimes there was no one to go to with an engineering problem. Getting in touch with Art was necessary. Art Collins had designed and built radios for his entire life, with the result that he knew exactly what he wanted and what he didn't. Everyone appreciated this so I spent a lot of time on an airplane between the two cities. It was better than guessing what he wanted and getting off onto the wrong track and then having to start over to please him.

It was rather strange how my experience as a pilot made those trips difficult for me at first. I was so tuned into the engine sounds and what should be done about them, that I didn't relax the entire time. I was busy flying the plane from my seat in the cabin. Later I learned how to sleep soundly even through dangerous actions of inept pilots.

I had made the right choice in going to work at Collins even though it paid less than my first job offer with the City of Glendale. That was a higher paid job with no challenge or I could go to Collins which was *all challenge* from morning to night. I decided on having interesting new things to learn about and I enjoyed it so much that I'd stay long hours and even week-ends rather than leave something unfinished.

I went home one late night to have Bev heat my supper while I went to the children's room to view them sound asleep. Back in the kitchen I told her that I found such satisfaction in what we were accomplishing at work that I didn't even need to get paid. I would do it for free.

She looked at me as if I had lost my mind and told me that she felt the same way about her job of raising children, but if one of us didn't get paid, the children would not do well without food and clothing.

I had to laugh. Of course I would continue to bring home a check. In fact, that brought up another subject. Next week would be the first of the month and I would be in Cedar Rapids. I wanted to see if she was willing to take over the job of paying the bills. It was a concern because she hated anything to do with numbers.

I had written out a list of bills due to be paid while I was away. On the other side I listed those that were due mid-month. I was paid twice a month and with three children, we were still living almost paycheck to paycheck.

I said, "If you follow this list and pay them on the dates listed, we won't fall behind when I am gone."

She just smiled and said, "You seem to have made it easy—all written down like that. Sure, I will do it. Where is the check book?"

I took the checkbook out of my pocket and gave it to her. That was the last I ever saw of it. I had just lost control of our money for the rest of my life. I was too busy to notice. But I would ask for some cash now and then, and still do, even though I retired 40 years ago. Bev keeps offering me the job back now, but she has always done such a good job of caring for our finances. Why change? She keeps very complete books of every cent that comes in and where it goes. She can tell me what we can afford and what we can't. I don't need to fix what is not broken!

Meanwhile, Art Collins had found a location for his new corporate headquarters in the town of Santa Anita, California. However, the City Council in its wisdom turned him down. At that time, the City Council thought that radio manufacturing was a smoke stack type of industry that they did not want in their city. They were unaware that the company's footprint would look like a well-groomed college campus and would bring significant tax revenues into the City.

Main Street, Richardson Texas 1950

Again Art disappeared for a few days and the next thing we knew was that he had chosen to put his new plant just north of Dallas Texas, in the tiny town of Richardson Texas. Construction got underway immediately and soon I had another location to fly to regularly.

Locally, Art was still not happy with the Burbank location where many of us were commuting to and from the San Fernando Valley daily, wishing he would hurry up and build on his San Fernando Valley property.

In 1959, our fourth child, daughter Bonnie Lou was born. Now we needed another bedroom. So we decide to buy a larger house very close to the property Collins owned in the San Fernando Valley, which was now surrounded by homes of other Collins families who like us were anticipating the plant to be built there. We sold the Pacoima house to Beverly's dad. He used it as a rental property. From Pacoima we moved to Granada Hills where we bought our dream house, five bedrooms, five baths, with room for horses in the backyard. There was a two-car garage with an apartment above. We lived there for about a year and a half before circumstances brought about our abrupt departure. We had not even completely furnished this large ten room house, when I learned that Collins was going to build the new plant in Newport Beach California, 50 miles south of where so many of his loyal employees had acquired homes.

Now what? Were we going to go to this new location and look for a different house down there, or keep our new dream house and find a different job? Suddenly fate took over. Overnight we were living in Tustin California in a rental unit ten miles inland from the new Collins plant being built in Newport Beach, California. We were fated to never return to our wonderful dream house again.

What happened was this: Pam came home from school one day and instead of playing outside with her pet animals like she always did, she said she was tired and needed a nap. Beverly checked her and said she was slightly feverish, as she was lying quietly on a small sofa in our wonderful new house. When I examined her I noticed a red rash. Soon she had that rash from head to toes. We called a local doctor. He came to the house and looked her over.

He said she had tuberculosis and must be moved at once to the Olive View Sanatorium and stay in isolation with other sick patients. I asked how he explained the rash—that was not typical of TB. The doctor went on to say that he was certain it was tuberculosis and if we did not take her to Olive View tomorrow, he would have the legal authorities come and take her. Without additional testing, he left.

I told Bev that Pam did not have TB but soon would, if we took her to that hospital. She must not go there! I was frantically thinking of any way to prevent this. I considered having Bev take her to Arizona and find a new doctor, while I stayed behind with the other children. But if authorities came they might arrest me if she was gone. Then they would take all of the kids. In other words, I had to do something fast.

I went to work early the next morning and inquired about a house the Company had just bought from an employee who had been transferred to Cedar Rapids. Ted Salyer, Vice President of personnel, who was trying to convince me to move to Newport Beach, told me I could immediately rent it and move my office to Newport Beach. He also said, "And if you like it, you can buy it. When do you want the movers?"

"At once," I said, "Today." A phone call later the movers were on the way. When I got home right behind the movers, the other children were all in school. The movers filled the van with everything in the house that we owned. We got the kids in the car, ready to go. We did not tell them why or let them see any friend, nor did we say goodbye to anyone. I locked up and hid the house key for a potential realtor hired by the company who would arrange for its sale.

As soon as the movers had moved everything into the new Tustin rental, we placed Pam in the master bed room with its own bath and told the other kids that they could only look at her from the doorway. I went to work the next morning. Bev enrolled everyone into a new school and then drove to Santa Ana with Pam to a large County Medical building. She explained our concerns and they gave Pamela a new doctor who took additional tests and after ruling out TB ran some more tests to learn what was causing her suffering.

It turned out to be something rarely reported in Southern California. It was called Rocky Mountain Spotted Fever, prevalent in the San Joaquin Valley and was associated with animals and carried by ticks. Now it is recognized as being in the San Fernando Valley area because it was so rural with horses, chickens and rabbits, along with cats and dogs, which expose people to ticks. Pamela lived in the separate room at the new Tustin house for three months then went to school fully recovered and healthy.

After working a while in Newport we bought a lot near Newport's Back Bay, by a fresh water lake called Cherry Lake, close to the Orange

Collins Radio Plant, Newport Beach, California circa 1959

County Airport and the new Collins facilities. I designed another dream house and we built it and grew to love the area and our new neighbors.

Sometime later when my son and I took up scuba diving, we bought some apartments on a beach front property called Fisherman's Cove in Laguna Beach California, which Bev managed as summer rents for the next thirty years. After I retired we moved into one of them where we have lived very happily ever since I left my last paying job.

I continued to work for Collins and our sudden move to the Newport Beach Plant gave me a good early boost with the Company. I was assigned as the functional head of digital switching systems for the company when Art reorganized it. I had a group in Newport and one in Texas. I flew to Texas for 3 days every week for several years participating in the company's projects and supervising engineering design. We were busy creating High Frequency (HF) and Very High Frequency (VHF) digital communications systems for the Navy, when the Korean War and Soviet cold war caused rapid expansion.

I spent a lot of time flying to the other two plants, even running an Engineering group in Texas by flying on the Collins Company plane, spending 3 days a week in Richardson Texas. The small plane was a Gulfstream turbo prop which carried up to ten people. The pilot and co-pilot were on standby for any company person who was needed somewhere else, unless Art Collins needed it first. Art decided that a private plane was needed after high-jacking of airliners to Cuba began to occur. It was no longer wise to carry classified (secret) documents on the commercial airlines. Art ruled that the Gulfstream aircraft on-board liquor cabinet had to stay locked up until 5 P.M. in the evening. Every Tuesday at 3 P.M. when we boarded the plane at Orange County (now John Wayne) Airport on our way to Addison Texas, we set our clocks to Texas time and opened the bar, however this did not work for the return trip on Thursday evening. I had so many things on my mind on the way to or from a job that I soon forgot to mentally fly the planes. I was a constant passenger who could even sleep sitting up. Sad to say, but by then the pilot in me had faded away.

When I first started at Collins in 1950, designing hardware in the Burbank plant, I was given the responsibility of completing the design of the Navy ARW-61, a VHF digital radio transmitter and receiver system to be used by the U.S. Marines. I completed Mel Doelz's original

Collins Burbank Office

design and took it like a baby to Washington DC Navy Laboratory for acceptance testing. It passed with flying colors. When I returned back in Burbank, Mel Doelz made me manager of Quality Control to oversee its production. I didn't really like that job because the very people who promoted me didn't like it when I actually kept tight control of the quality. Then I was made group leader of an Engineering Design Group that was developing equipment for the Distant Early Warning System (The DEW Line) communication link. This was a system of radars to make early detection of an incoming attack on the U.S.A. during the cold war with the Soviets or anyone who tried to send missiles at us by way of the polar regions. With the development of semiconductors, electronic design changed dramatically. Communication systems became more compact and needed less power. I became instrumental in helping the company make the transition to semiconductors

My favorite project, the one I am most proud of, was called the Navy Tactical Data System (NTDS). This was to replace the old tedious system where people manually kept track of the warships under the Admiral's command, using voice radio and writing data on a glass screens for him to know where each ship was located and if it was ready for action.

Collins Radio was challenged to produce a high frequency radio system for NTDS using secure encrypted ship to ship data links to keep track of a 300 ship task force within a 300 mile radius. Fleet vessels would routinely send status information regarding their location to the Admiral's flagship where it was quickly transmitted to an enlarged display, built by Hughes Aircraft Company, using a digital computer supplied by Univac, thus giving the Fleet Commander a constantly updated tactical fleet control and readiness system. The NTDS system was live "Beta Tested" at the San Diego Naval Electronics Laboratory with two ships underway in the nearby Pacific Ocean. They communicated over full duplex high frequency radios with the Laboratory located on

Point Loma, San Diego, designated as the Fleet Command ship. The Beta trials were very successful so the system was given approval to go into production for the entire Navy and is still being used today for fleet control all over the globe.

1960 to 1970 brought tremendous growth in electronics. The computer brought changes that were truly revolutionary. World-wide secure digital communications, nuclear submarine VLF/MSK secure message system, NASA and the Space program, automatic teletype store and forward systems, computer networking, digital communications modems for the internet, all had their beginnings. I was promoted to Director of R&D, Director of Engineering, and Assistant Vice President of Engineering of the Collins Information Science Center in Newport Beach.

These promotions were a bit strange because all the time Art kept after me to move my family to Texas. He said Texas was to be the center of the new Collins digital world. It looked like I would have to move to Texas if I ever wanted to be promoted to a higher corporate position. I chose not to move to Texas and take my chances. As I continued to insist on living in California, promotions slowly came my way

Collins Newport

anyhow. Sometimes if I got too personal, I would tell Art he should have made California the main center. His huge new boat was parked at the Balboa Bay Club in the Newport Beach harbor and he had the Newport Beach Office quietly working on new cutting edge systems. For years after he was gone the Newport Beach Office was still selling the things that were invented by our groups. They were outliving everything.

In 1971, Art Collins made the decision to expand Collins Radio into airline controls, computerized inventory systems, and other new markets employing digital technology. With this expansion, cash flow became an issue and Collins began a search for financial partner. Rockwell International joined with Collins, eventually gaining control and then firing Art Collins. That made me mad and I decided I didn't want to work for Rockwell so I "retired" and started a consulting practice. My life as a consultant was short-lived because I quickly realized I had four kids in or headed to college and not much money coming in.

In August 1972 I joined Actron Corporation, a subsidiary of McDonnell Douglas Corporation, located in Monrovia, California. Actron built avionics equipment for McDonnell Douglas aircraft. I was Vice President of Engineering for the McDonnell Douglas Actron Division. The division reported to Corporate Headquarters in St. Louis Missouri. At Actron we developed avionics systems for the Air Force F-15 being manufactured in St. Louis and the C-17 being developed in Long Beach California. We also developed high resolution cameras for the U-2 and SR-71 spy planes during the cold war.

In 1975 I started work with a new firm, Astrodata Co., where I was Vice President of Operations. There I worked on a system to automate teletype transmissions, which up to that time used a manual process of extracting a punch tape from a receiver and feeding it into the transmitter. We developed computer controlled teletype switching systems that were installed all over the world. We were using software and a computer control system from General Automation Company in Anaheim CA. The Plessey Company Plc, an English company, purchased Astrodata and I soon found myself involved in lots of international travel, going to different countries to help troubleshoot installations of the new equipment. Eventually they decided to move the whole plant to England. I was the last man out the door of Astrodata, as they asked me to handle a sensible, careful, shut down of U.S. operations.

In 1977 I joined Rockwell International in Anaheim, California. The main reason was that it was much closer to my home. (This was the same company that had bought Collins Radio). There we developed new wire line modems compatible with the U.S. telephone company switching network so we could send digital information to any dial-up phone—a big improvement over the old acoustic phone modems.

At an IEEE meeting I was approached by Anaconda Copper Company. They made me an offer I couldn't refuse to become Vice President of Engineering at a much better salary. They partnered with Atlantic Richfield Company (ARCO) to develop switching systems for rural areas to replace the old "party line" telephone system, where one telephone line served multiple customers. We developed a system of frequency division multiplexing so multiple calls could be handled simultaneously on one line. ARCO then partnered with the Ericsson Company, the large Swedish telecommunications company that pioneered cellular telephone switching systems. I was promoted to Vice President of Engineering. As the program expanded it was taken over by Ericsson and they brought in their own people. After several years of leading the industry, Ericsson's competition got up to speed and Ericsson began to leave the States and return everyone who wanted to go to Sweden with them or to jobs in other Ericsson offices.

I retired in 1985 after 40 years in the fields of electronics and communications. In hindsight, I was privileged to participate in many exciting new developments that laid the groundwork for email, cell phones, Skype and the Internet as we know it today. Those developments included:

- Development of high-frequency duplex communication systems (transmit/receive through a single antenna).
- Making the change from vacuum tubes to semiconductors, followed by developing large-scale integrated circuits and methods for their automatic manufacturing.
- Developing the first modem for converting digital data to a signal capable of being transmitted over wire lines or HF voice bandwidths.
- Working on encryption systems used in satellite communications and Very Low Frequency (VLF) systems for command and control of nuclear submarines.
- Improving telephone switching systems to handle multiple calls.
- Systems that eventually enabled the emergence of cell phones.

Looking back, I was lucky to have the jobs I had. I feel particularly fortunate to have worked with Art Collins, one of the true pioneers and innovators in the field of electronics. I loved my jobs. For much of the time I had so much fun I couldn't believe that I got paid to do what I did. One of my daughters summed up my career in three words:

"WW II to WWW"
(World War II to the World Wide Web).

Looking back on the equipment we had at our disposal as pilots in 1945, flying blind from one Pacific island to another, and comparing it to what pilots have today, the improvement is nothing short of miraculous. I think about the other young men of those days who would have come home alive if that equipment had been available back then. My grandchildren today have more information, more communication capability, more computing power, in their personal cell phones, then the entire Army Air Corps had in the South Pacific in 1945.

Bob and Beverly

Typical Family Gathering at Home in Laguna Beach, CA

CHAPTER 23

EPILOGUE

Bob: After returning from the South Pacific and being discharged from the Army, I served in the Air Force reserve for six years. I never realized my dream of flying over the Los Angeles Coliseum. In fact I never again flew as a pilot in command, although in my early 80s, I did go for a ride as a passenger in a PT 17 in Texas. However, my flying legacy became our kids. Our daughter Nancy married Peer Swan, a Vietnam helicopter pilot. Our daughter Pam got her own pilot's license after raising her four boys, Tripp, Grant, Andrew and John, all Eagle Scouts. She is now training for her instrument rating and belongs to a flying club at John Wayne Airport in California, flying small aircraft locally. Her son Grant attended the Air Force Academy in Colorado Springs and continues serving in the Air Force. Daughter Bonnies' second son, Cecil, flies charter jets all over the planet. Son Robert (JR) also became a private pilot, once having his own Cessna 172 at John Wayne Airport, but now has a Diamond DA-40 and his own hangar in Hidden Valley Airpark, Shady Shores, Texas.

When I graduated from Berkeley, (UCLA) as an EE, Beverly and I had three children, Nancy, Pam, and son Robert. Daughter Bonnie came later. At the time when I received my BSEE, I thought that Beverly should have at least received honorable mention of being the Mother of the year or something equivalent. At UCLA at that time the Graduate Student Association had a nice certificate they awarded to wives. It was the "PHT" degree, and stood for "Pushing Hubby Through." Although well deserved, I was busy working and never got Beverly her "PHT."

After retiring I planned to stay home and enjoy our beach. However, I did take up a number of civic activities. I participated in politics regarding various City Council issues. I worked hard supporting the North Laguna Neighborhood Association, I became active as the President of the City Parking, Traffic, and Circulation Committee and both Beverly and I served on the Laguna Beach "Friends of the Library" board. We participated in community service with local schools, Girl and Boy Scout organizations, the Hoag Hospital, and the Newport Beach Assistance League.

Beverly and I were fortunate that we did a lot of traveling, much of it when she accompanied me overseas on business trips. Our travels took us to Sweden (Beverly's favorite), England, Italy, Norway, France, Germany, Monaco, Belgium, Holland, Canada and Mexico, and the states of Texas, New York, Idaho, Utah, Montana, Oregon, Washington, Arizona, New Mexico, Florida and Washington D.C.

Beverly: Earlier I wrote how during the war my girlfriends and I worried that we might never get married. Wrong! Over the years, we stay-at-home girls continued to agree that being young mothers and wives, we were the lucky ones who had it all. We didn't regret a thing.

I only realized how young we actually were when my own daughters reached the age of 18 and continued on in school. They seemed to be putting off marrying until after getting a good education and were waiting on having children until they had time for those careers they worked hard to obtain.

Our old fashioned way had some advantages as I see it. With our early start we were young enough to enjoy being youngish grandmothers and now are still around for a darling new crop of babies called, great-grandchildren. How lucky can life get?

Speaking of luck, when I wrote about the Home Front (Chapter 3) I mentioned how I got a P-38 charm necklace. Over the years I've given some of my jewelry to each of my daughters. The P-38 necklace was given to my daughter Pam, when her son Grant had just been accepted by the Air Force Academy. I was happily surprised after Grant became an Air Force pilot when I saw that he was wearing that P-38 around his neck. Now Lieutenant Colonel Mizell, the P-38 has accompanied him through his nineteen years in the military, on every flight and in every combat zone, as a reminder and inspiration from the original tactical aviation generation. Grant began his pilot career flying the C-130

Hercules, accomplishing the same combat missions in Afghanistan, Iraq, Africa, and elsewhere that Bob did with C-47s in the Pacific. Grant continues to serve, now at the Pentagon in Washington D.C., representing Air Force interests to Congress and managing the budget on the C-130 fleet.

In summary, our four kids and their spouses (Peer, Jamie, Betsy and Randy) have given us fourteen grandchildren, of whom thirteen survive: Michael, Ashley, James III, (Tripp), Grant, Andrew, John, Libby, Scott, Mackenna, Jerome, Cecil, Clifford, and Kelly (girl). Sadly, we lost Bonnie's middle son Robert in a tragic accident. The grandchildren have so far added fourteen great-grandchildren: Beverly, Jake, Isabella, Victoria, Jadyn, Kyren, Hayden and baby, Kelly Christiansen (boy), Lorelei (Rory), Alex, Joshua, and Alexandria, plus Robert's second wife's child, Amy. Scott Mosier's baby, number fifteen is on the way." and we're happily still counting.

As Bob approached his 90th birthday, he was invited to take part in the Laguna Beach Patriots Parade. He was elected Patriot of the Year for 2014. This resulted in his picture being in the papers and periodicals and his being called by newspaper writers who wanted to know what it was like way back then. The American Legion wanted the younger generation to meet someone who lived through WW II, recognizing that there are fewer veterans every year. Bob spoke about being a pilot in the Pacific War, which many school age children of today had barely heard about.

Bob looks forward to finally becoming a published author before celebrating his 90th birthday in 2014. I plan to live to 100 and want him around for at least the next decade. I need an electrical engineer who can decipher all the remote controls we have for the television, VCR, stereo, and can restart my computer when the screen goes black and nothing works!

Beverly's P-38 Lucky Charm

APPENDIX

HOW TO FLY A TRANSPORT AIRCRAFT

The C-47 and C-46 transport aircraft described in this book were driven by two gasoline-powered engines. The larger plane, the C-46, had engines that generated 2,000 horsepower each while turning a 4-bladed 13.5 foot propeller. Today, transport aircraft are called "Airlifters" and have jet engines. The C-130, for example, has four turbo-prop engines, *each* producing over 4,000 horsepower. This means: heavier, higher, faster, further.

People wonder what it's like to fly an airplane. Many of today's pilots wonder what it's like to fly an airplane (since autopilot is often the one doing most of the flying). Much like the change in automobile technology from the 1940s until modern times, the airplane, how it is designed, and how it is flown has changed drastically since WWII. The purpose of this Appendix is to enlighten the non-pilot on flying, and honor those prop plane pilots who endured, rose to the challenge, and served their profession, many of whom made the ultimate sacrifice in the course of their duty. It also follows the aviator's "10% rule," meaning that any given part of the story is valid, so long as it's based on 10% truth.

The C-46 aircraft was powered by two Pratt & Whitney R-2800 radial piston engines. Modern aircraft are mostly jet engines, with the occasional turbo-prop, which is still a jet core but with a propeller geared to the front. The radial engine is similar to your car engine, in that it has pistons and runs through the same combustion process: injection of air and fuel, compression, ignition, and exhaust; or, in non-technical language: suck, squeeze, bang, and blow. The jet engine does a similar process, but continuously and with far more air and fuel and fewer moving parts, hence the reason for its use in modern aircraft. The jet engine is a long stack of rotating discs, the compressor (squeeze), the combustion chamber (bang), and the turbine (providing the mechanical energy back to the compressor). The air intake is accomplished by the huge hole in the front of the jet engine, and the exhaust is accomplished by the huge hole in the back. Numerous other parts, such as variable inlets, high-bypass fans, and articulating nozzles make the process more efficient, much like headers and turbo-chargers on a conventional engine.

This mechanical jargon above really means that the WWII radial engines emitted a deep, earth-shaking rumble, while the jet engine is often compared to a whining noise (no one quite knows which whines louder, the engine or the copilot). The WWII radial engine gives off the smell of gasoline, burnt oil, and crew chief man-sweat and leaves its shiny mark in puddles on the tarmac, while the jet engine runs on jet fuel, smelling like kerosene lanterns at a summer camp cook-out. On the same note, the radial engine pilot has to be one with his engines, sensing their every need and heeding their every cough and sputter. The radial engine pilot must continuously be vigilant in case the engine needs a little more gas, a little less prop pitch (just a hair), or in case it suddenly decides to blow an oil seal or burst into flames. The jet pilot has computers that do all that stuff for him, leaving him complacent about the aircraft, but far more attentive to the flight attendants and in-flight rations (What's for lunch?).

The pilot always walks around the aircraft before getting in and starting it up. This gives him one last opportunity to see popped rivets, loose bolts, open hatches, fluid leaks, or, in the case of the radial engine, a lack of a fluid leak (indication that you're out of fluid). Further, in a WWII aircraft, the walk-around gives the pilot time to fill his zippo lighter from the fuel tanks. The jet pilot should not do this, firstly because jet fuel does not light in a zippo, secondly because smoking is not allowed onboard modern aircraft, and lastly because the Transportation Safety Administration (TSA) would promptly confiscate his lighter. After the walk-around, the modern pilot programs the computer, downloads necessary route and weather information, and asks the computer if all the aircraft systems check out. The radial engine pilot gets his map out and stuffs it under his leg for future use, checks the wind by placing his index finger out the window, and taps on the old gauges until they unstick and come back within limits.

Finally behind the yoke (the device that controls the attitude of the plane), even a task as rudimentary as starting engines has its nuance. The modern jet pilot checks the dials and makes sure the computer isn't reporting any abnormalities, then presses the engine start switch and watches the gauges flash and move until either the engine is stabilized, on-speed, or the computer auto-shuts down the engine for a problem. If the latter, the pilot returns the aircraft to maintenance and heads in to the lounge for a coffee. The WWII radial engine pilot checks the cross-wind and temperature, as these could cause a hot start. He nods to his crew chief, who stands near the prepared engine nervously, shifting back and forth while clutching a fire extinguisher. After once again checking all required lever positions and reviewing that the parameters are within limits, the pilot actuates the hand-driven fuel pump, not so quickly to flood the engine, but enough to build starting fuel pressure. Actuation of the engine starter must be done with care and released as soon as the engine catches, so as not to shear the starting shaft. As the engine begins belching, banging, rattling, backfiring, and spluttering, flames and black smoke shoot about three feet out the exhaust pipe. Moments before the pale fire-guard commits to pulling the extinguisher pin, the engine "catches." When the pilot feels that instant of smoothness, he moves the fuel mixture to full rich, calming the flames and transitioning the exhaust to white smoke. Much as this color calms the revelers in St. Peter's square when a new pope is chosen, the white smoke cues the chief that all is once again right in the world and he can move to the other engine for another harrowing ordeal. The rumbling of the first engine gives the pilot's gut a massage, sending him to his comfort zone, while it rattles the instrument panel enough that the novice merely sees a blur of gauges without enough fidelity to determine the status of the second engine's start.

With engines running, the taxi pattern of the two differ, mainly because the modern aircraft has "tri-cycle" gear, or rests firmly horizontal on the main wheels and the nose wheel, while the radial is a "tail dragger," sitting on two hefty main wheels and a small castering tail wheel. The modern pilot steers by way of a "tiller," or small steering wheel that works much like your car. The tail-dragger takes direction from the brakes, a separate one for each side, controlled by pushing on the top of each rudder pedal. Further, the tail-dragger pilot must S-turn, weaving back and forth across the taxiway as he goes. The nose of the aircraft points up in the air, so the only way to see is out the side window. The dance continues all the way to the runway, a little left brake, look out the window, a little right brake, look out the window.

Once on the runway, a jet pilot, especially one with the Full

Authority Digital Engine Control or FADEC, throws the throttles to the wall and bolts down the runway. The FADEC ensures that the engine stays within limits and supplies the pilot with the right amount of power. The radial engine requires more precision. Advancing power too quickly could result in an over-temperature (generating enough heat to melt some of the engine components), an over-torque (the propellers producing so much twisting force that it damages the engine or wing), or an over-pressure (trying to put so much power through the engine that the head blows off a cylinder). Further, the propellers not only generate forward thrust, but some forces called spiraling slip stream, p-factor, gyroscopic effect, and torque effect. The spiraling slip stream spins the air around the aircraft in the same direction as the propellers, bouncing air off the tail, pushing it right, and therefore the aircraft nose left. This requires the pilot to compensate with a boot full of right rudder. Next, p-factor, or the tendency of the downward moving blade of the propeller (typically on the right side of the engine on American models) to push more air than the upward moving blade when the nose is up, also causes a pull to the left, requiring more right-rudder compensation. The gyroscopic effect acts 90-degrees to the force applied on the gyroscope (the engine), so when the tail-dragger lifts the tail, the gyroscope pulls left. Yet again, right rudder. Finally, torque follows Newton's Third Law. The engine spins clockwise (looking forward), so the aircraft tries to spin counter-clockwise. To correct this, the pilot must hold--you guessed it, right rudder. When all is said and done, the pilot leg-presses between 100 and 200 pounds to keep the aircraft running straight down the runway. The faster the aircraft goes, the more air flows over the rudder, therefore the more the pilot can relax. A failure at slow speed can be catastrophic, and plenty of pilots have lost their aircraft and crew to a misapplied rudder.

Once airborne, the pilot can finally relax—if he has the latest autopilot. Above 10,000 feet, meal service can start and the pilot's iPad comes out while he monitors the radios for pertinent air traffic control messages. The C-46 pilot, on the other hand, rarely makes it to 10,000 feet. Levelling at 8,000 feet, the radial engine pilot adjusts the six levers controlling pitch, throttle and mixture. The pilot must synchronize the levers to keep the engines running at approximately the same speed, at the same pitch, or else suffer the dreaded "prop beat," a vibration that fatigues both the crew and passengers in short order. The pitch lever determines whether the propeller blade is flat (producing no thrust, but allowing the engine to spin freely) or feathered (taking a huge "bite" of air, but also excessive resistance on the engine) or somewhere in between. The pitch lever is too high if the engine speed bogs down and too low if the engine runs away. Of course, this is closely tied to the throttle. More gas equals more RPM, but also a higher temperature and pressure (just like your car). Too much gas takes the engine beyond its red-line and not enough stalls the engine. Finally, mixture changes the fuel-air ratio in the engine. More air, or a leaner engine, causes it to burn hotter and more efficiently, until there is not enough fuel to maintain the explosion, resulting in a starved engine. Too much fuel wastes gas by dumping it out the tailpipe, unburnt. The radial engine pilot becomes the master of manipulation of these three levers as a side-show to his manhandling of the actual aircraft controls, the stick and rudder.

At altitude, with props synchronized, navigation becomes the key activity. In a modern aircraft, this means setting the GPS, autopilot, then listening for any air traffic control (ATC) directions or aircraft generated alarms. In the WWII aircraft, it meant pulling out the map and compass. Right after departure, the pilot might get a few minutes to head to the back and use the relief tube, but with a constant ear to the sound of the engines, listening for any early sign of trouble. Upon returning to the cockpit, the pilot guestimated the wind and aircraft drift, then set his heading by use of the magnetic compass. Over land, the pilot always kept a list of nearest airports or good "off field" landing locations, like a long straight road or the field of a local farmer with an attractive daughter. Over water, on the other hand, was a different beast altogether. Over open water or at night, the engine makes all sorts of new noises. The pilot's ears became super human, noticing pops and sputters that were never there before. Every cylinder fire echoes through the pilots head, keeping him scanning at the engine instrument stack to reassure him that failure isn't imminent. While mortal humans, tied to the ground, might experience rain and clouds, the pilot flies above the clouds, looking down on the silver and pink hued billows and basking in the sunshine or starlight. Of course, navigation without GPS becomes more challenging. Even with a ground based beacon or AM radio station, which the aircraft can tune up and get a heading to, any lightening has a tendency to pull the pilot's compass and direction finding needle off course. In particularly bad weather, the needle jumps left and right erratically, and the pilot must use the TLAR method of heading choice, otherwise known as "That Looks About Right." When the pilot sees the wall of clouds ahead with lightening flashing inside, he makes a calm call to the back so the passengers can tighten their seatbelts. Up front, he frantically ties down anything that was previously unsecured, as turbulence has a tendency to toss even the heaviest objects into locations that cause the most damage. The subsequent roller coaster ride is better than any amusement park and reminds you that airshow pilots aren't all that special, as even a simple thunderstorm can make an aircraft fly sideways or upside-down. The pilot merely holds on for dear life and attempts to keep the aircraft somewhere between space and the ground. Hitting either would make the ride come to an abrupt ending. Once out the other side of the weather, the pilot notifies the passengers and lets Air Traffic Control know that there's slight turbulence on route. He then scans the airplane to count the number of popped rivets and see if all the major parts are still attached. If the controls still work and the gauges show within limits the pilot can go back to navigation, and attempting to determine how far off course he drifted and if there's still sufficient fuel to make his destination. Honestly, we should feel sorry for modern pilots, as they must work so much harder to avoid dozing off due to their extreme boredom.

Finally, if fortune, wind, and skill all converge on this lucky day, the pilot arrives overhead his destination and prepares for landing. Landing in a jet requires the pilot to fly straight in line with the runway at approach speed, then, over the runway, cut the power and drop like a rock onto the landing gear. He applies brakes, reverses thrust, and uses the nose wheel steering tiller to stay in the middle of the runway. Landing a prop requires finesse, body english, excessive pumping of the rudder, a lot of nerve and prayer. The tail dragger has to keep his wild mustang inside the corral. Even small crosswinds try to push and pull the plane off the side of the runway, darting anywhere it darn well pleases merely taking the "suggestions" of the pilot into account, or not. After gross manhandling of the controls, and often more than a few curse words, the pilot brings the aircraft to a reasonable taxi speed and exits the runway at an appropriate place.

Only after pulling into the chocks and shutting down can the pilot relax. He turns the aircraft back to his crew chief, regurgitates the endless list of things wrong with the airplane, which need to be fixed before tomorrow's sortie, and heads off to the bar while the chief plans another all-night work session.. In the bar, the pilot's first drink is to steady his nerves, the second is to whet his windpipe, and the third is to magnify his good looks. After the first three, the subsequent drinks only serve to embellish the recount of harrowing scenarios from which he gallantly saved the aircraft and passengers. He must tell all stories tonight, for tomorrow he will do it all over again and the dice may roll differently.

With thanks to Lt. Col. Grant Mizell

RETURN AT YOUR LEISURE

St. Patrick's Day 1998 we were invited to Santa Anita for a day of Horse Racing. St. Patrick's Day meant just one thing to me... the day I was drafted long ago in 1943. Waiting for Beverly to finish getting ready, I called her to get my green tie. The just-delivered mail, I dropped on her desk. A single letter was addressed to me in pencil. Bending closer, I looked it all over. No return address. Opening the envelope, I was surprised to find an old yellowed envelope tucked inside addressed in my own hand writing to a school friend I had not seen for years. I didn't remember ever even writing to him, but obviously I had. A little yellow sticky note was attached to the envelope with a short explanation.

"I found this in my mother's garage as I was cleaning it out for her. It was in a shoe box full of old stuff I had left behind. I re-read your letter and as embarrassing as it was, decided to mail it back to you." —Rich.

What could possibly be embarrassing? A photograph fell out on the table, THAT I did remember, a picture of my first plane crash.

A pilot in training in Arizona, I had my first experience with engine failure and was trying to get back to the airfield to land. However, a mile or so short of the landing strip my plane came down in the open desert. My copilot cadet Moskowitz and I both got out with just a few scratches and stood waiting to be rescued. My memory recalls the cactus flying by the windows, as we went in wheels up, but I had no idea who took the picture. I was too worried about what this would do to my chances of becoming an Army pilot. Would a crash wash me out? The plane was totaled. The Review Board called it a vapor lock in the fuel system and I went on to earn my wings. A couple of days later, someone handed me the photograph of the damaged plane. No people were in the picture. As I re-read my letter to Rich, it seemed that I told him about the crash, dropped the picture into the envelope and added a postscript:

"This is the only copy I have of this picture, so please return it at your leisure. Thanks —Bob."

I laughed looking at the post mark from the Army Base in Douglas, Arizona. More than *fifty* years had passed since I sent him this letter. I was still laughing when Bev brought me my green tie. I must remember to thank Rich for returning my crash photograph...the next time I see him, say in the next fifty years or so. (photo p. 14)

ANNOTATED BIBLIOGRAPHY

Bradley, James. 2003. *Flyboys: A True Story of Courage*, New York: Little Brown and Company. This is an unforgettable story about American flyers that had the misfortune to be captured by the Japanese on Chichi Jima Island. They were executed and horrible atrocities committed on them. President George Bush was shot down here also, but was saved when he was picked up by a submarine.

Brines, Russell. 1944. *Until They Eat Stones*, New York: J. B. Lippincott. The author is an Associated Press correspondent who was imprisoned with his family by the Japanese, first in the Santo Tomas camp outside Manila and later in Shanghai. He documents the Japanese militaristic philosophy and how it affected the conduct of the war.

Campbell, Tom K. 2006. *Tokyo Trolley: Memoirs of WW II In the Pacific.* Jackson, TN: Main Street Publishing. The author flew troop carrier planes in the Southwest Pacific, beginning on the island of Biak and continuing through the Philippine and Okinawa campaigns until the Japanese surrender.

Chase, Gen. William C. 1975. *Front Line General—The Commands of William C. Chase.* Houston: Gulf Publishing. General Chase tells what it was like to take part in the capture of the Philippines, including his successful rescue of the 3,700 civilian internees in the Santo Tomas camp.

Daws, Gavin. 1994. *Prisoners of the Japanese: POWs of World War II in the Pacific.* New York: Quill/William Morrow. A detailed treatment of POWs captured by the Japanese in all theaters of the Pacific War including extensive interviews.

Dos Passos, John. 1946. *Tour of Duty.* Boston: Houghton Mifflin. Describes visits to Philippines and Guam near end of war, including a trip to meet Philippine guerillas.

Drury, Bob and Clavin, Tom. 2007. *Halsey's Typhoon: The True Story of a Fighting Admiral, an Epic Storm, and an Untold Rescue.* New York:

Grove Press. From December 16 to 19, 1944, a severe typhoon battered the American 3rd Fleet under the command of Admiral William Halsey. It was east of the Philippines, guarding MacArthur's right flank during the invasion of Mindoro. Three ships were sunk, numerous others damaged, and 793 sailors lost their lives.

Flanagan, Edward M. 1999. *The Angels Came at Dawn*. Novato, CA: Presidio Press. In a daring raid behind Japanese lines, paratroop infantry dropped by Troop Carrier Squadron aircraft rescue civilian POWs from the Los Banos camp.

Kahn, E. J. Jr. 1962. *The Stragglers*. New York: Random House. This book describes the stories of a number of Japanese stragglers on Guam, the Philippines, and other Pacific Islands, how they survived (some resorted to cannibalism) and their reluctance to surrender.

Manchester, William. 1978. *American Caesar: Douglas MacArthur 1880-1964*. Boston: Little, Brown. Biography of General Douglas MacArthur and his background and plan to liberate the Philippines.

Hylton, Wil S. 2013. *Vanished: The Sixty Year Search for the Missing Men of WW II*. New York: Riverhead Books (Penguin). On September 1st, 1944, a group of B-24 bombers took off from Wakde Island, Dutch East Indies for a bombing run on Palau. The targets included Peleliu and Koror. One plane was shot down and three parachutes were observed to open and land in the sea before the plane crashed near Koror. The fliers were captured, taken to the island of Babeldoab, and beheaded by the Japanese Kempeitai (Secret police) in retaliation for the bombing.

Mosier, Jack Arthur. 2013. *Jack*. Bakersfield, CA: Self-Published. This autobiography of 144 pages describes the Mosier family through the eyes of Jack Mosier, Robert Mosier's older brother. After his honorable discharge from the Army, Jack earned a PhD and worked for the State of California Department of Education.

Mosier, Robert R. *Letters, 1943-46*. Lt. Mosier's letters home contained a wealth of detail about the operations of the 57th Troop Carrier Squadron except for matters (such as locations) that were censored.

Mosier, Robert R. *Flight Logs, 1943-46.* Lt. Mosier's flight logs describe dates, destinations, missions flown, type of aircraft, hours flown and landings made.

Pennock, John H. 1945. *Saga of the Biscuit Bomber: With the 57th Troop Carrier Squadron in the Southwest Pacific Theater.* Sydney: Halstead Press Pty Ltd. This short book describes the activities and personnel of the 57th Troop Carrier Squadron. The author was the squadron's intelligence officer.

Pennock, John H. 1944-46. *57th Troop Carrier Squadron Monthly History Reports.* These are monthly reports prepared by the Squadron Intelligence Officer for submission to the Commanding General, US Army Air Force, Washington D.C.

Savary, Gladys. 1954. *Outside the Walls.* New York: Vantage Press. An American woman married to a French man managed to stay out of the Manila prison camps so she could aid the prisoners. Description of life in Manila under the Japanese occupation and during its recapture by American forces, with the freeing of the POWs in Santo Tomas on February 3rd, 1945.

Sides, Hampton. 2001. *Ghost Soldiers.* New York: Doubleday. This is the story of a daring raid behind enemy lines on January 30, 1944 by General Walter Kreuger's Alamo Scouts and the Sixth Ranger Battalion to liberate 512 POWs in the Cabanatuan POW camp near Manila.

Sledge, Eugene B. 2007. *With the Old Breed at Peleliu and Okinawa.* New York: Ballantine Books. Arguably the best book ever written about island combat in the South Pacific, Sledge, who went by the nickname of "Sledgehammer" as a Marine enlisted man, describes the horrors of war. The Marines and Infantry had 1,794 men killed and over 8,000 wounded or missing in taking this small island to protect MacArthur's flank as he moved on the Philippines. After the war many questioned whether the sacrifice was even necessary.

Smith, Craig B. 2012. *Counting the Days: POWs, Internees, and*

Stragglers of WW II in the Pacific. Washington D.C.: Smithsonian Books. This book tells the story of six POWs. Three were Americans, imprisoned by the Japanese, and three were Japanese who became prisoners of the Americans. All had amazing survival stories.

Smith, Robert R. 1961. *The United States Army in World War II—The War in the Pacific: Triumph in the Philippines.* Washington, DC: U.S. Government Printing Office. This book documents Japanese army battle plans and American offensives leading to recapturing the Philippines.

Smith, Robert R. 1952. *The United States Army in World War II—The War in the Pacific: The Approach to the Philippines.* Washington, DC: U.S. Government Printing Office. This book describes MacArthur's island hopping campaign (New Guinea, Wakde Island, Biak Island, Noemfoor Island, and Peleliu Island) as the stepping stones to the invasion of the Philippines.

Stearns, Ben W. 2002. *Arthur Collins: Radio Wizard.* Marion, Iowa: Ben W. Stearns, Publisher. This biography of Arthur Collins describes how a teen-age ham radio enthusiast went on to become one of world's leading experts in high frequency radio communications. Collins radios became the standard for WW II aircraft and after the war the company pioneered many new digital communication technologies.

Zuckoff, Mitchell. 2011. *Lost in Shangri-La.* NY: Harper Perennial. Near the end of the war, a C-47 on a sightseeing junket crashes in a remote New Guinea valley. There are only three survivors—one of them a WAC. Their rescue by troop carrier glider is an amazing story.

END NOTES:

To the greatest extent possible, I have used contemporary source material for this book. I wrote a number of letters home to my mother while overseas and she kept them for me. Where quoted, I note the source and date as follows: *Ltr RM to MM, June 10, 1945.* A second important source was all of my original flight logs, both while undergoing flight training and then later while in the South Pacific and in Japan, until I was finally released to go home. These records I obtained from the Department of Defense when I began working on this book. I used this notation when referencing my flight logs: *FL, June 10, 1945.* A third important source was the monthly 57th Squadron History Reports. These were submitted to the Commanding General, Army Air Forces, Washington, D.C. They described operations, squadron moves to new locations, promotions, demotions, accidents, and aircraft operating statistics including tonnage flown, fuel consumed, etc. In most cases these reports were prepared by Captain John H. Pennock, the squadron intelligence officer. I note these as *Sqd Hist, Feb p 3.* I would like to acknowledge the kind assistance of Lt. Col. Grant A. Mizell, USAF, who assisted me in obtaining these reports. The notation used for referencing these reports is: *57th Squadron History, June 1945, p.6,* and so on. Other references are listed in the bibliography under the name of the author.

1. Pennock, J. H. 1945: p 67

2. Flight training report, 1944

3. FL, Oct 45

4. FLs Oct-Nov 1944

5. Mission Report Nov 44 p 3

6. Sqd Hist, Dec p 3

7. FL Dec 44

8. Sqd Hist Jan 45 pp 3-4

9. FL Jan 45

10. Sqd Hist, Feb 45 p 5

11. Zuckoff, M. 2011

12. Sqd Hist, June 45 p 7

13. Sledge, 2007

14. Smith, Craig B. 2012, p 212

15. Sqd Hist Jan 45 p 5 (1st Lt Ralph C. Eckels, Acting Unit Historian)

16. Kahn, E. J. p 79, and 84. He also describes stragglers from other areas of the Southwest Pacific; a dozen that surrendered on New Guinea in the early 1950s (p 96, 105).

17. Kahn, E. J. pp 125-147

18. Sides, Hampton 2001

19. Chase, General William C. 1975

20. Flanagan, E. M. 1999

21. Savary, Gladys 1954 p 190

22. Savary Op cit p 187

23. Campbell, Tom. 2006 p 72 reminded me what the highway looked like.

24. FL Feb 44

25. Months later I saw an article in Colliers magazine that described how we came in and flew out some of the POWs (R. Mosier).

26. Ltr RM to MM Feb 24 and Nov 9, 1945

27. Sqd Hist Feb 45 p 6

28. Pennock J. H. 1945

29. Ltr RM to MM Apr 17, 45

30. Sqd Hist Mar 45 p 8

31. FL May 45

32. Ltr RM to MM May 30, 45

33. Sqd Hist Mar 45 pp 4-6

34. Sqd Hist May 45 p 3

35. Sqd Hist, May 45 pp 3-4

36. Sqd Hist June 45, Appendix III

37. Sqd Hist July 45 p 6

38. Sqd Hist July 45 p 8

39. Ltr RM to MM Jul 10, 45

40. Bradley, James 2003 p 218-248

41. Op. cit. pp 192-197

42. FL Aug 45

43. Ltr RM to MM Sept 8, 45

44. Sqd Hist Aug p 4

45. Ltr RM to MM Sept 18,45

46. See www.mansell.com, "Center for Research, Allied POWs under Japan/ Hokkaido Island POW Camps

47. FL Sept 45

48. Ltr RM to MM Sept 11, 45

49. Ltr RM to MM Oct 11, 45

50. Drury, Bob and Clavin, Tom 2007

51. Ltr RM to MM Oct 25, 45

52. Ltr RM to MM. Sept 30, 45

53. The DUKW was designed in a collaboration between famous yacht designers Sparkman and Stephens and General Motors. The initials in the name have the following meanings: D, designed in 1942; U, Utility vehicle; K, front wheel drive; W, 2 powered rear axles. It could travel at 50 mph on land and 5.5 knots in the water.

54. Smith, Craig B. 2012 p 30. This was where Kazuo Sakamaki, midget sub commander, trained before attacking Pearl Harbor

55. Ltr RM to MM (Nov 2, 45)

56. Stearns, Ben W. 2002 pp18-20, 26-27

ACKNOWLEDGEMENTS & CREDITS

I gratefully acknowledge the assistance rendered by my grandson Lieutenant Colonel Grant Mizell, United States Air Force, Washington, D.C., who helped me obtain information concerning the Troop Transport Squadrons activities in the southwest Pacific campaigns of WWII.

I cannot thank Ms. Yvonne B. Kinkaid enough for her diligence and perseverance. Ms. Kincaid is a historian at the USAF Headquarters, Pentagon, Washington, D.C. She did an outstanding job of searching through seventy year old records—often nearly unreadable microfiche copies—to uncover critical dates, and events that helped fill in the gaps in the manuscript (and in my memory)!

Many thanks to Andrew Mizell, another of my ten grandsons, for organizing the maps that are included in the book. With his skillful drawing ability he has given the reader a good overview of the specific, island to island, combat areas that the U.S. Forces followed as we advanced towards winning the war with Japan.

I gratefully acknowledge the assistance of my daughter Nancy Swan, who designed the cover and book layout, and daughter Pam Mizell who helped review the manuscript.

I also appreciated the help and encouragement of all the other family members who kept after me to finish writing the war stories that I had verbally related to them over the years.

Finally, thanks to Craig B. Smith, who pulled this document together. He undertook an editing job and became a lifelong friend.

We gratefully thank the following individuals or organizations for permission to reproduce photographs: photos no. 1-12, 14, 15, 28, 30, 31, 39, 66-68, and 74-76, courtesy of Robert R. Mosier family; photos no. 18, 22, 25, 26, 29, 33, 35, 47, 49, 51, 58 are reproduced from Pennock, J. H., 1945 *Saga of the Biscuit Bomber: with the 57th Troop Carrier Squadron in the Southwest Pacific Theater*; photos no. 11, 20, 46, 48 U.S. Air Force photos; photo no. 16, from www.navsource.org/archives/09/22/22139.

htm; photo no. 19, www.USArmymodels.com /articles/ rations/10in1 rations.html; photos no. 32, 37, 38, 40, 50, 52, 59, 60, 62, 64 from: Tennent, G. J. and Fox, M. J., *Displaying Australia and New Guinea*, Australia Story Trust, Sydney, 1945, acknowledgements to Literary Licensing LLC who reprinted the book; photo no. 34, thanks to 508th Parachute Infantry Regiment, www.508pir.org; photo 61, from Appleman, Burns, Gagler, & Stearns, *U.S. Army in WWII: Okinawa: The Last Battle*, p 418, Army Center of Military History, Washington, D.C., 1948; photos no. 41, 42, 43, 44, 45, 54, 55, 56 courtesy of John Tewell. Mr. Tewell, living in Manila, has compiled an extensive album of historic photos of the Philippines. These can be accessed at: https://www.flickr.com/photos/johntewell/sets/72157625790065191/; photos 53, 63, U.S. Department of Defense WWII Photo Archives; photo no. 65; U.S. National Archives, RG 306-NT photo no.70, en.www.wikipedia.org/wiki/Richardson_Texas; photos no. 69, 71, 72, 73 courtesy of Rockwell Collins Corporation.

FOR COMMENTS OR INFORMATION:

info@docksidesailingpress.com

Index

Symbols

10 in 1 Ration Illustration 33
10 in 1 rations 41
57th Troop Carrier Squadron vii, xiv, 28,
    29, 32, 40, 45, 56, 64, 68, 69, 85,
    104, 123, 194
    Chart Troop Carrier Wing 35
    Poem: Forgotten But Needed Men 60
375th Troop Carrier Group vii, xiv, 32,
    40, 82, 104, 121, 134
    WW II LOCATIONS OF THE "TO-
    KYO TROLLEY" 40

A

Actron Corporation 173
Aircraft
    C-46 viii, 36, 45, 64, 84, 86, 91, 104,
        106-108, 123, 128, 132, 133, 181,
        184
    C-47 vii, viii, xii, xiv, 26, 27, 29, 31, 32,
        35, 38, 39, 41-45, 55, 58, 59, 63,
        65-67, 69-71, 73, 76, 88, 91, 93,
        94, 103, 107, 109, 181, 192
    P-38 vii, ix, xii, 21, 178, 179
    P-47 vii, 31, 46, 107, 108
    PT-17 12, 153
Air Medal ix, xiv, 89, 134, 140, 143, 146
Atsugi, Japan 122-125, 127, 129-132
Atsugi, video of first landing 125

B

Biak Island v, vii, viii, 24, 27, 32, 35, 37,
    39, 40, 45, 47, 49-51, 56, 57, 59,
    60, 62, 64, 66-68, 72, 73, 74, 76,
    77, 89, 90, 96, 107, 189, 192
Biscuit Bombers xiv, xv, 28, 33, 96, 191
Bob and Other 57th Squadron Pilots 32
Boroke Airfield, Biak 45
Brisbane 29, 95
Bush, George H. W. 114

C

C-46 viii, 45, 64, 84, 86, 91, 104, 106,
    107, 108, 123, 128, 132, 133, 181,
    184
C-47 vii, viii, xii, xiv, 26, 27, 29, 31, 32,
    35, 38, 39, 41-44, 45, 55, 58, 59,
    63, 65-67, 69-71, 73, 76, 88, 91,
    93, 94, 103, 107, 109, 181, 192
Camp Stoneman 5, 29
Chichi Jima Island 189
Chitose Japan 127
Christmas Island vi, 29
Clark Airfield vi, viii, 40, 104, 105, 107,
    109, 110, 113, 120, 125, 135, 137,
    198
Clifford, F. W. 57, 109, 150
Collins, Arthur vi, viii, 40, 104, 105, 107,
    109, 110, 113, 120, 125, 135, 137,
    198
Collins Radio Company ix, 144, 162,
    163, 165-173
Corregidor 64, 82, 88, 101, 104
Crystal Beach Gang vii, 4, 57, 149, 152

D

Dobodura xii, 40, 94
Doelz, Mel 170, 171
Douglas Arizona vii, 5, 13-15
Douglas DC-3 71
DUKW ix, 138, 196
Dulag 81, 82

E

Elmore Field Mindoro 104

F

flight log 45
Floridablanca viii, 108
Fort Stotsenberg 120
Fuzzy Wuzzies 30

G

General R. E. Callon troopship 15
glider tows 24, 64
Griffith Park Observatory 3
Guadalcanal 21, 25-27

H

Hastings, Margaret 70
Hiroshima Japan ix, 116, 123, 124, 134, 138, 139
Hokkaido Japan vi, 127, 130, 196

I

Ie Shima Island ix, 115
Iwo Jima Island 114

J

Jack Mosier vii, xi, 1-4, 23, 112, 141, 146, 158, 163, 190
Japan 145, 146
Japanese viii, xii, 3, 5, 17-19, 21, 25-27, 29, 30, 38, 39, 45, 49, 50, 52, 59, 61- 63, 65, 68, 72, 73, 77, 78, 82, 83, 85- 87, 89, 93, 100, 106, 110, 114, 117, 119, 120- 125, 127-133, 136, 138, 139, 189-192. *See also* Stragglers (Japanese)
Japanese surrender 119, 189

K

Kadena Airfield vi, xii, xiv, 26, 38-40, 65, 73, 77, 78, 80, 83, 85, 105, 114, 116-118, 121, 123-125, 127-132, 134, 140, 142, 145, 146, 194, 196, 197
Kearns Field Utah 11, 15
Kennedy, Joe 100, 132- 134
Kibbe, Russ 60, 151
Koganei Country Club Japan 136

L

Lae 31, 38
Landfall method (of navigation) viii, 74

Laoag Airfield 137, 138
Leyte 45, 46, 56, 64, 80- 82, 104
Lubang Island 73, 100-102
Luzon vi, 40, 68, 82, 83, 104-107, 114, 137, 146

M

MacArthur, General Douglas 39, 62, 68, 72, 80-82, 85, 121, 130, 146, 190-192
Maps:
New Guinea, Biak, Pelelieu, Philippines 29, 34
Okinawa to Japan 116
Philippines to Okinawa 80
Western U.S. Pilot Training Command Locations xvi
Marston matting 28
Milan, Kenny 100
Mindoro Island 40, 56, 64, 80-83, 85-87, 90, 99, 101-104, 190, 198-200
Minter Field CA 5, 13
Morotai Island 45, 78

N

Nagasaki Japan 116, 119, 124, 134
Nasuno airfield 129
Nazab Papua New Guinea xii
New Guinea v, vii, xii, xiv, 15, 24-32, 35, 37- 41, 45, 46, 58, 61, 65, 68, 70, 74, 90-92, 94, 97, 98, 146, 192, 195
Noemfoor Island 45, 192

O

Okinawa v, vi, viii, ix, xiv, 23, 39, 40, 80, 105-107, 110, 113, 114, 116-121, 124, 127, 130, 132, 134-138, 140, 189, 191
Owi Island 45

P

Papua New Guinea xii, 28
paratroopers xii, 31, 60- 62, 65, 68, 70
Peleliu Island v, 71, 72, 89, 192

Pennock, Capt. J. H. vii, viii, 37, 96, 191, 194, 195
Philippines v, viii, 14, 39, 45, 56, 64, 72, 81, 85, 88, 89, 98, 100, 101, 104, 120, 124, 137, 140, 146, 189-192
Porac Luzon vi, 40, 68, 104, 105, 107-109, 112
Port Moresby, New Guinea xii, 26, 29, 32, 38, 40, 90, 91, 94
POW camps (Cabantuan, Bilibid, Santo Tomas, Los Banos) 85, 127
PT-17 12, 153
Pyle, Ernie 114

Q

Quezon Avenue 86

R

Randolph Field Texas 5, 15, 44
Reid, Charlie 100, 136
Rockwell international 172, 173

S

Salyer, Ted 168
Samar Island 64
San Jose Mindoro v, 40, 81-83, 86, 90, 99, 101, 104
Santa Ana Army Air Base 11
Santo Tomas POW camp v, viii, 84-88, 189, 191. See also POW camps (Cabantuan, Bilibid, Santo Tomas, Los Banos)
Santo Tomas, Video Air Rescue 88
SAVANNA (weather code) 128, 137, 138
Shangri-La 68-70, 192
SS William C Sublette 57
Stragglers (Japanese) 190, 192
Sydney Australia 33, 36, 50, 90, 94

T

Tachikawa Japan vi, 40, 116, 121-123, 131, 132, 136
Tacloban 45, 46, 56, 64, 81, 82
Tarlac Luzon 135

Tokyo Trolley 31, 104, 121, 122, 124, 134, 189
Townsville 29, 95
Troop Carrier 26, 27. See also 57th Troop Carrier Squadron; See also Biscuit Bombers
Typhoon (Cobra, Louise, Halsey's) xiv, 118, 119, 130, 132, 135, 190

U

UCLA 154, 157, 158, 177
University of California Berkeley 158, 159, 161, 177

V

Video, Atsugi first landing. See also Atsugi, video of first landing
Video, Internees Santo Tomas. See also Santo Tomas, Video Air Rescue
Vincit Qui Primum Gerit 27

W

WAC 69, 70, 112, 135, 146, 192
Waco gliders 65-68
Wakde island 27, 68, 91, 190, 192
Wau Airstrip viii, 27, 92, 93
Wewak 38
Wickenburg Air Force Base 5, 11, 44, 152
Willis, Bill 96, 97, 100
World Wide Web 174

Y

Yontan Airfield Okinawa viii, 105, 137

Made in the USA
San Bernardino, CA
12 September 2016